A MATTER OF SPIRITUAL CUSTODY

BY BARRY STEVEN ROFFMAN

RAINBOW BOOKS

A MATTER OF SPIRITUAL CUSTODY
By Barry Steven Roffman

Cover by Marilyn Ratzlaff
Produced by Ratzlaff & Associates
Published by Rainbow Books/Betty Wright
P. O. Box 1069
Moore Haven, Florida 33471

Printed in the United States of America
ISBN: 0-935834-55-9
Library of Congress No. 88-43165
Price: $15.50

TO MY FAMILY

And he shall turn the heart
of the fathers to the children,
And the heart of the children
to their fathers;
Lest I come and smite the land
with utter destruction.

MALACHI 3:24

CONTENTS

PREFACE

"Steve Robinson" is a man with a plan, a man with political aspirations that center around the State of Israel. He has, ever since 1976, worked to alter the doctrines of earth's major religions in an effort to advance the cause of peace. He has already enjoyed a limited degree of success in relations affecting Jews and Catholics. It is hoped that this work will further his cause in the area of Jewish-Moslem relations.

The story that you are about to read is true. It deals with one of the most unique custody bouts in history. Although I have often been asked to use the actual names of the protagonists, I have opted for a style that employs pseudonyms for some in an effort to provide a measure of privacy for those involved. The historians or the curious may learn their real identities easily enough by looking up the news clippings cited, which are real and which may be found in the microfilm sections of appropriate libraries.

The Catholic Church has, in recent years, been struggling to overcome allegations of collaboration with the Nazis. The press has, at times, been full of stories concerning war criminals that were given refuge within the walls of the Vatican itself. Possibly in response to such charges, Pope John Paul II has attended synagogue in Rome, a first for any pope. He has also made more than one trip to the extermination camps to pray for the victims, although (until his meeting with Jewish leaders in Miami on September 11, 1987) he has found it easier to speak of all the "people" rather than "Jews" murdered there. It is true that there were millions of non-Jews gassed and burned (including Catholics who gave their lives in an effort to save Jews), but most victims were Jewish; and the prime thrust of the Nazi effort was the total extermination of all Jews on earth. Although it gives minimal solace to the survivors, knowledge that Christendom grieves the actions of some of its members in name at least serves to help reassure a justly nervous Jewish people that what has repeatedly happened before will never occur again. To deny or overlook the particularly Jewish nature of the Holocaust is to give comfort to those who now seek to deny the slaughter of two thirds of European Jewry.

In a controversial gesture on May 1, 1987, the Catholic Church beatified Sister Teresa Benedicta of the Cross (formerly Edith Stein), a convert from Judaism who died at Auschwitz in 1942 after her church refused to make a serious effort to save her and other Catholics "of Jewish blood." This action, however, was quickly followed by a meeting between the pontiff and Austrian President Kurt Waldheim, an accused Nazi war criminal. No effort was made by the pope then or in a 1988 meeting between the two to condemn the Austrian for his record; but John Paul II did praise the man as "always dedicated to securing peace among peoples." Some papal apologists have suggested that it was a "Christian" act for the pope to forgive Waldheim even as he had forgiven the man who made an attempt on his own life. Indeed, the pope has the right to forgive his assailant if he so chooses. He does not, however, have the right to forgive those who have thrown over a million children into the ovens. More, while the Vatican had signed a Concordat with the Third Reich on July 20, 1933, and though its current pope has met with Arafat and Waldheim, it still fails to recognize the State of Israel and maintains the Catholic position that Jerusalem, the Heart of the Jewish people, be carved out of the Jewish state and made into an international city. The full normalization of relations between the Vatican and the Jewish people can never be achieved until Rome reverses its policy on the above two key issues.

Not withstanding the above mixed bag of developments, the case described herein represents a positive turning point in relations between the Catholic Church and the Jewish people, even if there is reason to question the Church's motives for ruling as it did. Catholics, who are already beginning to teach about the Church's role in the Holocaust, are asked to reflect on the evidence presented herein. Perhaps their pressure and the collective good will of Christianity's largest branch can be enough to complete the reforms at times hinted at by John Paul II.

There are really two custody stories contained herein. One, already bathed in the light of the press, is about "Bobby," the product of a modern, broken mixed-marriage. The other is about a piece of land . . . known as Temple Mount. For the past two millennia, the world has been waiting for the drama of this second custody battle to be played out on the stage of Jerusalem.

Fundamentalist Christians see the reconstruction of the Temple as a prerequisite for the return of Jesus. The Jews, rejecting him but not the hope of a Messiah, view the reinstatement of the Temple and concomitant sacrificial rites as part of the more important Messianic Age. The Temple must be rebuilt upon the current site of the Dome of the Rock Mosque, Islam's third most holy site. This fact serves to tie the three great monotheistic faiths together, for it is only an accord between Jews and Moslems, backed by Christians, that can lead to the fulfillment of all which has been prophesied.

Mr. Robinson asks that Israel trade some, but not all, West Bank and Gaza land for a promise of non-intervention by the Arabs that will allow for the building of a new Temple. If his plan succeeds, then we may indeed see Isaiah's vision of peace finally fulfilled in our time.

— I —
THE PILGRIMAGE

Steve Robinson loved to take his two year old son to the beach on Key Biscayne. This time, however, was different.

"Bobby," he said with a lump in his throat, "Daddy is going far away. I still love you, and I'll come back to visit as often as possible."

The boy's only response was to cling tightly to his father. Steve tried to rationalize that ever since his legal separation from Carmen five months earlier, he had been given little time with his son anyway.

The night before his flight to Israel was a restless one. The thirty-year-old bearded Jew kept seeing his son's face. It didn't help to rationalize about how difficult it was for a man to gain custody, or about the fact that his lawyer had told him to not even waste money thinking about it. He felt guilty about running off and leaving the boy like that. When the sun came up, he had changed his mind about a permanent move but was still determined to go away for a while to calm his nerves and sound out the ideas espoused in his new book, *The Great Christ Debate, A Quest for the*

Theological Reconciliation of Judaism, Christianity and Islam. There was irony in the subtitle for religious differences between Steve and his mother-in-law had been behind the marital breakup. The problem with getting access to Bobby would have to be put on hold until his return, as only in the Middle East could he learn whether or not the publication of his work would prove worth the price he had paid: his home and marriage to the lovely Puerto Rican model, Carmen Rodriguez.

On April 3rd, 1979, having taken a leave of absence from his teaching job and armed with about two hundred copies of his new book, he checked in for El Al's inaugural flight from Miami to Tel Aviv.

The trip was unlike any other he had experienced before. Steve found himself joining a group of Hasidic Jews for evening prayers in the aisles soon after the plane was airborne, and, though not a daily habit, he donned tephillin (Biblically prescribed prayer boxes bound to the head and arm by leather straps) with them the following morning.

The sun came up with the plane somewhere over Spain. As the azure Mediterranean sped by below, he could sense a growing anticipation. "Aliyah" is Hebrew for "going up" and there is a feeling on a flight to Israel that one is indeed "going up" to be nearer to the Almighty Himself.

At last, after what seemed like an endless flight, the coast of Israel appeared. Cheering broke out among the 350 passengers, but Steve was disappointed with his initial glimpse of Tel Aviv. Except for pollution rising from a power plant below, the scene was much like the Miami Beach he had left behind. What he wanted wasn't a jet flight to another modern resort, but a time machine to whisk him into the distant past, to the very roots of his people.

On landing, he was hard put to find a cab or limousine driver willing to haul his small library to Jerusalem. A well-tanned Sephardic driver, however, agreed to help him for fifty dollars, a small fortune to most Israelis.

The ride from the airport initially didn't lift his spirits because much of the terrain was reminiscent of the farm lands of New Jersey, which he had always seen as depressing. But with time, the land began to rise and take on a more rocky appearance. The highway was dotted with wrecks left over from past wars. Each of the tall pines that lined the road seemed to beckon the limo on to greater heights and to point the way to the City of God.

Finally, Jerusalem itself was in view. He could make out a few mosque towers; and as the limo made its way through the city, there were occasional glimpses of the old city's wall that he had sketched in his mind and heart countless times before.

Exhausted, he got a cheap room at the old Orgil Hotel, a somewhat beat-up place that was easy on his budget. Too tired to tour, he dozed off for a while. When he awoke at night, he could see the lights of the Old City. It was an inspiring sight, but loneliness kept him from enjoying it as much as he thought he might. The nearest human he knew was on the other side of the world and already he was missing his son, even though he had been seeing the boy only four hours per week before he left.

At daybreak he put on a warm flight jacket, took two copies of his book, and after a quick breakfast, set off on foot for the Old City. At the instant he entered the walled-in town through the Damascus Gate, he felt that he had found his time machine. Arabs rode about on donkeys. Spices filled the air. The Muslim call to prayer could be heard as a sea of tourists and religious pilgrims pressed to make their way through the crowded market place. Only the Uzi machine guns sported by so many Israeli soldiers served notice that he was still held captive by the twentieth century.

After wandering through the colorful bazaars, he found an exhibit portraying the Shroud of Turin in the Christian Quarter of the city. (*DISCOVER MAGAZINE* would later, in October, 1982, reveal that there were iron oxide and vermilion paint pigments as well as collagen tempura, a popular Middle Age binder on the reputed burial cloth of Jesus, and a 1988 Carbon 14 test would eventually confirm Bishop Henri de Poitiers' 1357 pronouncement that the shroud was indeed a forgery).

"I'd like to have someone here read and react to what I've written," he told the museum curator.

"Your subtitle is quite ambitious," the Christian said.

"Even so, please read it with an open mind."

The man agreed. Steve was pleased to have found a reader; but the thrust of his book was directed more at Islam, so he headed for the Dome of the Rock Mosque. It was, however, Friday, the Muslim Sabbath, and Robinson was unable to get in.

Not knowing what else to do, he decided to call Mirium Levine. Steve had never met her before but had dated her sister in Miami.

"Steve Robinson?" Mirium replied over the phone. "Of course I know who you are! Karen wrote me all about you several times. She seemed to be impressed by your book.

Do you have an extra copy?"

"Only a few hundred. Of course you can have one. In fact, I need someplace to store them while I tour the country."

"No problem, I've got room here," she said and added, "Can you come over for dinner tonight before the Sabbath starts?"

"I'd be delighted to. Would six be OK?"

"Six will be fine. Bring some Kosher wine if you can."

Steve arrived at her place just before sunset. He was a bit let down by what he saw. Although he wasn't exactly the handsomest man in Israel, he had a penchant for beautiful women. Mirium was a frail-looking woman with thick glasses. She offered a certain inner charm, but he couldn't help comparing her to his estranged wife; and though Carmen had given him no reason to hope for a reunion, he had yet to accept that fact. Nor had he seriously pursued any new love.

The woman refused to let him leave after dinner. It was Friday night and the buses weren't running anyway. Almost nothing moves in Jerusalem then, and she didn't want him to violate his first Sabbath in the Holy City. As it was, Steve seemed to need someone to unload his problems on. He showed her about a dozen pictures of Bobby, then told her his life's story and about how it had come to pass that he had married Carmen. Mirium quickly learned why Carmen's "Born-again" Catholic mother (Theresa) had worked to destroy her daughter's marriage after reading his controversial new book on Jesus.

"It sounds like you really hate Theresa," Mirium noted.

"Actually I used to enjoy discussing things more with

her than I did with my wife," the writer answered. "For years while she thought there was some hope for converting me, she was a pleasure to have around. In fact, she even lived with us for a while. But when Bobby was born, Carmen and I entered him into the Jewish Covenant with a brith milah at his circumcision. A year later Theresa demanded that he be baptized Catholic. Things got nasty. I threw her out of our house, bags and all."

"I'll bet that did wonders for your marriage," Mirium quipped.

"Quite," Steve answered. "Still, I never thought Carmen was serious about pulling out. I assumed Bobby would be enough to keep us together. What a mistake. Now I've got to figure out how to get him back."

The two stayed up talking until 3:00 A.M. Sleeping on the sofa that night, he felt relieved to have found a friend.

That Sunday Robinson set out for the Dome of the Rock again. During the walk to it he decided to tour the Church of the Holy Sepulcher at Golgotha in the Christian quarter of the Old City. The church is built over the alleged site of the Crucifixion.

A Muslim guarded its entrance. The church itself was divided up into five regions, somewhat symbolic of the division that reigned after the life of Jesus. There were painted border lines to show the territories of the Roman Catholic, Armenian Orthodox, Greek Orthodox, Abyssinian Coptics and Syrian Orthodox Churches. A lack of agreement between the various sects kept the place from having any single architectural style though the mixture seemed to be primarily Frankish and Byzantine. The building had twice been destroyed by earthquakes, once in the

12th century and again in 1927. Learning this led Steve to wonder whether or not that would be the way the Dome of the Rock Mosque would eventually fall to pave way for the Third Temple.

After visiting Calvary in the church, he was surprised to find that the tomb where Jesus is said to have been laid to rest was in the same edifice only a few dozen feet away. Entrance to it was via a double set of low openings, each designed to make the visitor bow when entering. The inner one was lower than the outer. Muslims went in backwards to keep from worshipping someone they did not consider to be God. Not wishing to offend the Christians, nor wanting to worship the "Christ," Robinson bent sideways when entering (an easier task at the outer opening than at the inner one). A Christian, stationed next to the marble slab on which the famous body may once have lain, asked for a donation. Steve gave none, pretending to not notice the fellow. Instead, aware of the Babylonian Talmud Sanhedrin's charge that, "Jesus the Nazarene practiced magic and led Israel astray," he examined the room to see if Jesus might have found escape possible. There were windows present. The ones in the outer portion of the tomb were too small for Robinson to fit through, but there was a larger window in the inner room that was covered by a portrait of Mary. Although the window was closed most (but not all) of the time he was there, the portrait covering it did appear to be large enough to allow for an escape and, although he was unable to learn exactly when the window had been put in, the fact that it was there at all only served to increase his skepticism.

On finally reaching the Dome of the Rock Mosque, a

sign at the base of the staircase leading up from the Jewish Quarter of the Old City warned that rabbinical law prohibited Jews from touring Temple Mount. The Holy of Holies, site where the Presence of God was once manifest in the form of a thick cloud, was somewhere up there. Steve thought about the edict for a minute and then dismissed it. "If the rabbis allowed Gentiles to walk all over the place, and they aren't defiling it, then why should I?" he thought. Anyway, he wasn't about to miss a chance to visit what was pictured on the cover of his book.

On the Mount he toured the Mosque and walked around, then under the rock on which Abraham offered to sacrifice Isaac. A guide pointed to where Muslims sav Mohammed ascended to heaven.

When the tour was over, he asked an attendant where he might go to discuss *The Great Christ Debate*. The man didn't comprehend English but understood when he saw Steve's portrait on the book's back cover.

The writer was taken to the library on the Mount. There an Arab sent a messenger to inform the Mufti, Muslim leader of Jerusalem, that an author friendly to Islam was in their presence.

The Mufti was a thin man, about fifty years old, perhaps older. He wore a red fez on his head and he spoke no English. An interpreter was summoned.

"As-sallaam Alakum," Steve began. "I'm a Jew but I'd like to help resolve a few of the differences that divide us. I believe Mohammed was, like our prophets, divinely inspired so I keep much of Muslim and Jewish Law."

"Do you want us to do likewise? If not, why do you keep both?" the Mufti asked.

"No, I obey both only as a token of my life's ambition, ending the hostility that divides the two halves of our common family."

"An admirable goal, my friend," the Arab said, "I'm happy that you apparently accept our Book, but I must inform you that it was sent to replace Torah. You need only follow our law."

"I don't agree." Steve answered. "The Koran was sent in Arabic for the sons of Ishmael. The Torah was given at Sinai for the Jews, the sons of Isaac. Each law is valid for the people who have received it. What we need isn't bloodshed over our differences, but a healthy respect for them."

The Mufti argued that Jews had corrupted the Torah, even as the Christians had corrupted the Gospels, but asked his guest to continue. The remark, however, caught Steve off guard, for he had seen much in the Koran to back the Torah. He hesitated before continuing, thinking to himself, "Can this man be serious?" Robinson knew that the Torah makes no effort to cover up the shortcomings of Moses or the sins of the Jews, something which could be expected had it been politically altered.

"I understand," Steve told the Mufti, "why you say that the New Testament was corrupted. That view and the distortion of Jesus' doctrine by Paul are cornerstones of my book. Ancient manuscripts like the Sinaiticus and Vaticanus are quite different from many modern versions of the New Testament. Even within a given translation today there are big differences in how Jesus is quoted from Gospel to Gospel. The four Gospel resurrection stories often contradict each other on important details. Most of what's found in the King James Version of Mark's resurrection account is reduced to a mere footnote in the Revised Standard Version because modern scholars believe the section to be a hoax. But I have never seen any evidence that would indicate the Jews have acted in similar fashion with the Torah."

"If the Jews had not altered their Scriptures, they would have accepted Mohammed," the Mufti said. "Tell me about *The Great Christ Debate.* Why have you written it?"

Steve wanted to argue more about the integrity of the Torah, but decided that it was best to advance the conversation towards his main reason for coming to the Mosque.

"My wife," Robinson answered, "is Christian and it was for her and the son of our mixed marriage that I began a search for the truth about Jesus some three years before.

"In Judaism today our most important prayer, the '*Shema*', declares the Unity, not the Christian Trinitarian, nature of God. I learned that Jesus taught the same thing in Mark 12:29. In John 4:22 he even said salvation comes from the Jews (i.e., the Jewish teachings about God and Law) and that God is not a man, but a Spirit. Again, on the cross he declared, 'My God, my God, why have YOU forsaken ME?' All this seemed to point to a historical Jesus not in conflict with the basic tenets of our faith. He never thought of himself as God."

"So far we agree. Continue," the Mufti said.

"Christians think Jesus claimed to be Divine because he said 'I and my Father are one.' But in the seventeenth chapter of John he prayed that the disciples might be one, even as he was one with the Father. This meant he had to be speaking about unity of purpose with God, not unity of identity!"

"Certainly," the Muslim said, "if Jesus called himself

the Son of God, a fact that we question, he also said, 'Call no man your father on earth, for you have one Father, who is in heaven.' Why therefore haven't you Jews accepted him as a prophet as we have?"

"Jews," Robinson answered, "haven't accepted Jesus because we saw him as a blasphemer. We also thought he opposed Jewish Law. Yet he said, 'Whoever relaxes one of the least of the commandments and teaches men so, shall be least in the Kingdom of Heaven.' We've confused Paul's anti-law position with the views of the Nazarene. And we rejected him because of his fulfilled promises in Matthew 10:34 and Luke 12:51 to bring the sword and division as opposed to peace, the expected role of the Messiah."

"Why do you think he would make such a strange promise?" the Mufti asked.

Steve replied, "The answer, I believe, was given to us by Mohammed. He told us:

> 'To each among you God prescribed a Law and an open way. If God had so willed He would have made you a single People, but His plan was to test you in what He has given you: So strive as in a race in all virtues. Your goal is to know God better. In the end when you return to Him as we all must, He will show you the truth of all things that you now dispute.'

"Jesus was sent to test us. The question is, will we fail God's test by focusing on our differences or will we pass it, as Mohammed has suggested, by focusing on our common moral tenets? Surely as the Koran teaches us, God will resolve our differences when we die. Our task then, as Jews and Muslims, isn't to war on each other, but to show the world the way to true peace. The Nazarene told us how to attain that goal. The Kingdom of God, he said, is within us. *US*! Not some magical Messiah! When we want it badly enough, it's ours for the taking."

"Be specific," the Mufti sighed. "How can we achieve this Kingdom of God that our prophets have spoken of?"

"By making a simple trade. A Third Temple for the Jews and a Palestinian state for the Arabs in exchange for it. God told Mohammed to change the qibla, the direction a Muslim faces in prayer from Jerusalem to Mecca. Did you ever wonder why?"

"I suppose you have an answer from Allah Himself to give us?" the Muslim said euphemistically.

"Perhaps," Robinson asserted, "it was to tell the Muslim that he must seek spiritual fulfillment through the haj or pilgrimage to Mecca, not Jerusalem. It is in Mecca that the Muslim makes his sacrifice. But God has decreed that it is in Jerusalem that the Jew must make his. Help us to attain our spiritual fulfillment. Let us build our Temple and fulfill the sacrifices that God has ordained for us in our Law. I believe that in exchange for a pledge of non-intervention by the Muslims of the world, the Jews would gladly give up enough of West Bank and Gaza territory to allow for a Palestine State. In short, we will trade a nation for a Temple."

"This holy place is ours!" bellowed the Mufti.

"You know," Steve said, "the Nazarene is quoted in Matthew as having said:

> 'If you are offering your gift at the altar, and there remember that your brother has something against you, leave your gift there before

the altar and go; first be reconciled to your brother, and then come and make your gift.'

"The Bible shows that the first murder occurred when Cain slew Abel. The motive was jealousy by Cain over Abel's offering. It's time for the sons of the brothers Isaac and Ishmael to stop killing each other. Abraham's descendants should never be in the business of impeding the other's offerings to God."

"Mr. Robinson," the Mufti said with a half chuckle, "I like many of your ideas. But the Jews don't believe that our Book is from God. We would never give up our possession of the Mosque here until they accept the Koran. And then we won't have the need! They can worship here as Muslims! And even if they accepted the Divine revelation of our Book in principle while they still continue following the laws of Torah as you advocate, would you really expect us to leave our beloved Mosque completely?"

"Who's House is the Mosque?" Steve asked. "Yours or God's?"

"God's most certainly!" the Mufti answered.

"Then as God loves all His children, He would never want you to leave completely. Isaiah (66:21) taught us that He would indeed want you to stay on, even in a priestly capacity."

The Mufti reflected for a moment on all he had heard, then finished by saying, "Go, convince your stubborn fellow Jews of what you've told me. If you succeed, then we'll have something more concrete to talk about. Please leave us a copy of your book. I wish you well. As-sallaam Alakum, Mr. Robinson."

"Alakum Wa-sallaam," Steve replied. That ended the

encounter.

The writer was excited by the meeting. Too excited. He walked down into the Jewish quarter and then started through the Dung Gate to leave the Old City when he was suddenly stricken with an intense chest pain. He dropped to the ground and lay there for about ten minutes, short of breath and in fear of a heart attack. Was God now punishing him for having violated the Holy of Holies? His mind was bombarded by a rash of fears. He began to think carefully about all that had transpired that day. It wasn't just that he had tread upon forbidden ground. He had failed to adequately defend the honor of the Torah when the Mufti impugned its faithful reproduction down through the ages. If he had missed something in the Koran that attacked the validity of the Torah, then the premise of his aspirations and his work had to be wrong. Mohammed might not be the prophet sent to correct what (from the Jewish perspective) had been Paul's destructive work. Perhaps, he thought, this was what God was trying to tell him by frightening him so. The pain then receded and he managed to hail a cab for a ride back to the hotel. He resolved not to go into the Dome of the Rock again.

"I need a better answer about my work than the Mufti or his friends can provide," he told Mirium that night over the phone.

"What are you going to do?" she asked.

"Go to the Source, to Sinai. I don't know what I'm going to find there. Probably just a bunch of hot sand and rocks. I do know that I haven't found what I'm looking for here."

Steve spent a restless night back in his hotel. He kept

dreaming about Bobby wearing a little sailor's hat. Over and over again he would hear the boy call out, "Daddy! Daddy!"

"How can I bring life into this world," Steve thought, "and then run off like this?" He knew that his son would soon start to worry that he would never return. Then, because the boy was so young, Steve feared that Bobby would forget him completely.

On Monday Steve borrowed a backpack from Mirium to set out for the journey to Mount Sinai, then under Israeli occupation. It was Passover that week, and Mirium had warned him that he'd be unable to get a hotel room in Eilat where he would need to pick up a guided tour. Steve couldn't be persuaded to stay in Jerusalem. He was the kind of man who always had to have things his way, and he had not yet learned to heed advice from others when it was contrary to his will. Anyway, he thought, "Moses didn't hesitate to march toward the mountain of God for lack of hotel space. Why should he?"

There were two reasons for the trip to Sinai. Here Moses and Elijah had spoken with and heard from God. Perhaps it was still His "home" on earth. Steve hoped to ask the Almighty whether *The Great Christ Debate* was or was not divinely inspired. He also wanted to appeal for another not-so-small miracle, the return of his son.

The bus from Jerusalem to Beersheva was packed. Almost half of those on board were Zahal (Israeli Army personnel,) and a good number sported Uzis or other weapons. What impressed Steve the most was that nearly all of the female Army members on board were beautiful. Israeli women, he soon noticed, were much prettier and healthier looking than American Jewish women.

He tried to change buses in Beersheva to get to Eilat, but all seats were sold out days before and it was useless to wait around. There was nothing else to do at first but stroll through the market place where he saw people shop for the night's chicken dinner. Unlike the States, shoppers here selected their poultry while still alive. Steve watched the slaughter of a few birds, then discovered that for not too much more than the price of a bus ticket, he could catch a sherute, a kind of limousine, to Eilat.

There were six other passengers who shared the ride. Most of the trip from Jerusalem to Beersheva had been boring, except for the women he had seen. Now the journey grew far more intriguing. They passed by the nuclear power plant at Dimona where Israelis allegedly make nuclear weapons, then descended into the Negev desert. The colors of the rocks were spectacular as the sherute dropped ever further below sea level. They could see the Dead Sea, a bright blue mass that was absolutely flat. Upon reaching the basin the view became more monotonous. Occasionally the sherute would drive through a sand storm which would reduce visibility to near zero.

Eilat reminded him of Las Vegas. Not that there were any gambling casinos, but here where desert terrain collides with a cold tongue of the Red Sea was a modern resort. Steve spent the late afternoon walking to every hotel in town. He even tried the youth hostel, which was a real flop house. No luck. There wasn't a bed to be had anywhere; and despite his earlier brave words, he was now wishing that he had listened to Mirium. He was carrying a large sum, and although most of it was in traveler's checks, he wasn't anxious to sleep on a crowded beach. There was, however, no other choice.

The beach was packed with partying Israelis all night. Most had tents and cooking gear. Steve had only his backpack for a pillow. He was unable to sleep at all. At one point he got up and took a walk toward the Jordanian border. On a barbed wire fence a sign said that there were mine fields just ahead. The lights of Jordan's port Aqaba were only a mile or two to the east.

He turned north at the border and started to walk inland. It was pitch dark and it seemed like a good place to have a talk with God. As he began a monologue, hoping that he was alone with the Almighty, troops armed with machine guns rushed at him from out of the darkness. "My God," he yelled, "Don't shoot! Ahnee Americanee! I'm American!"

It was an Israeli border patrol. "This isn't a safe place to take a stroll," a young sahmal (sergeant) told him. "Please continue your walk back at the beach."

The following morning he succeeded in getting an expensive room at the Queen of Sheva Hotel. Exhausted, he decided to spend another night in Eilat before continuing.

In the afternoon he set out along the beach again in the direction of Aqaba. "This," he thought, "was the Holy Land. Was it too much to expect God to give him a favorable omen? Did God approve of his trip, or was He too busy to care?" Then, oddly enough, he noticed water in a stream feeding down into the Gulf of Eilat that was almost a perfect blood red. It looked like the plague of the Nile was being repeated just for him. Perhaps, he cautiously thought, it was red clay beneath the water which produced the eerie effect.

He scooped up a sample in a Coke bottle, and it was indeed crimson. Gazing out at the sea he saw that all was blue except for an area of about a thousand square meters where the stream ran into the Sea. There the waters were red. Was this, he wondered, the sign he had sought?

While the pilgrim was a very religious man, he was also a science teacher and his training in that area caused him to challenge initial impressions. He asked about the red water everywhere, but nobody could explain it or tell him if perhaps it was red algae from a fish farm inland someplace. One man told him he thought it was treated sewage, but he wasn't sure.

The following morning Steve joined a group by the youth hostel that was headed for Sinai. The guide (Ari Ben Jacov) was a rugged looking, brash young Sephardic Israeli who boasted of sexual exploits from previous expeditions. There were two young Swedish girls in the group to ensure that his record was kept intact. Also along for the journey was a Dutch honeymoon couple and an English Protestant minister.

The first part of the trip down the Sinai coast was fast, easy and breathtaking. They stopped to view the coral island with its Crusader fortress, then at a fjord. After diving at the reef near Nuweiba, and competing with swarms of flies for lunch, they turned inland and the modern highway was soon replaced by sand and rocks (today the highway goes all the way to Mount Sinai and then on to Cairo). At a high point just upon entering the desert the sweeping panorama seemed to stretch back through time, and Steve found himself searching in vain for millions of his wandering forefathers and for Moses.

It was April, but it was already very hot. The group drove on at a painfully slow speed for what seemed like an eternity. Ari showed them ancient Hebrew writings on rocks just south of the desert path, then took them to a 5,000-year-old ruin that included the oldest roofed buildings in the world. The structures all had windows facing roughly west. They were tombs. It was possible to date the exact time of the year for the death of each person buried there because the window for each tomb pointed to where the sun set on the day of the burial.

As the group continued, it seemed that there was nothing but sand and rock for as far as the eye could see. Then, in the midst of nowhere, they passed a Bedouin. The Arab had his head pressed down against the sand as he prayed towards Mecca. A camel was with him, but nothing more. Another 20 miles passed before they saw another sign of human existence.

In the late afternoon the expedition reached a Bedouin encampment where the travelers paused for tea under black tents. The nomadic Arabs were most hospitable. Ari spoke fluent Arabic, and it was obvious that the guide was their good friend.

The group spent the night at another Bedouin encampment about five miles from the foot of Mount Sinai. The grandeur of the mountains by now was most gripping. Somewhere out there he knew, God had appeared long before and had given his people the Torah. Millions of fellow Jews had heard His voice. Was it too much to ask that one more Jew would be so privileged here?

Ari cooked up a stew for dinner over an open campfire after everyone had taken their turn peeling potatoes, carrots and onions. It might have been because he was so hungry, or perhaps because some flavoring of the manna from heaven was still in the air, but Steve had never enjoyed a meal as much before.

When darkness ruled the heavens, he stood in awe of the star field which was so rich that only the blackness of jagged peaks could reveal where sky caressed earth. The awesome beauty and tranquillity of his surroundings convinced him that God must still be near.

The group tried to sleep until about 1:30 in the morning, then rose under the now ascended full moon to complete the trek to the Mountain of God.

After a half-hour drive, they arrived at the Santa Caterina Monastery located at the foot of Mt. Sinai. The Greek Orthodox structure was built some fifteen hundred years ago. Because of its isolation, its monks hadn't learned of the occurrence of World War II until 1948.

Everybody started the climb together at just past 2:00 A.M., but the group was soon completely divided by the physical conditioning of the climbers. Steve took the lead, not wishing to share his initial experience at the summit with a pack of tourists.

At first the climb up the "Snake Path" was gradual and not too tiring. The moon was soon poised over the peak of the mountain. High cirrus clouds crowned it with a halo ring and moonbeams lit the jagged rocks ahead, often giving an almost surrealistic impression of angels standing in the way of his ascent. With each step up, the vista expanded and he felt that he was all the closer to God. Two hours into the climb, he reached the "staircase to heaven," built centuries ago by the monks who then lived below. It consisted of huge cut stones. The angle of climb was now much steeper, about forty-five degrees, and the ascent was increasingly difficult. Steve had run marathons before. He wasn't sure which was harder.

The summit was reached only fifteen minutes before sunrise. He found a small Greek Church and at the peak a room that served as combined synagogue and mosque. Just beyond it was a sheer drop that had to be nearly a mile. There, on the precipice, he began his prayer to El Shadai, the Almighty. When he was finished he yelled, "Shema Olum Adonoy Elohaynu, Adonoy Echod," a modification of the central prayer of his faith. His version meant "Hear, oh world, the Lord our God, the Lord is One." The standard Jewish version addresses "Israel" rather than the world, something that Steve felt was too narrow a message. His prayer echoed twice off the surrounding mountain peaks before silence ruled again. Not long after this, the first of the tourists arrived and his chance to hear from God was over.

He stayed for about an hour. Many was the night that he had imagined this place when he could not sleep. It was one way to overcome his frequent insomnia. Now he wanted to fix the true image firmly in his mind.

Not having heard a reply from God, he started down the mountain feeling the very reverse of the emotions that had spurred him on to get to the top. The climb had taken just under four hours; the descent was over in an hour.

At the base of the mountain, he toured the monastery and gave the head monk a copy of his book for the library, the second largest theological collection in the world (the Vatican has the largest). When he arrived outside the monastery, one of the Swedish girls was sunbathing topless.

During the trip back to Eilat he realized it had to be a miracle that two million Jews could survive for forty years in a place like the Sinai desert. There seemed to be almost no water anywhere, as was evidenced by the cakes of dirt (and flies) that covered the Bedouin he had encountered.

The tour finished up in Eilat that night. Feeling compelled to see all of Israel before returning home, Steve began a three-week journey riding buses to every corner of the land. The only place that troubled him was Tel Aviv. As a Jew, what disturbed and embarrassed him the most about it was the tolerance of explicit pornography in public places (especially at the Egged Bus station). He had never really thought much about the issue elsewhere, but felt that his people were defiling the Holy Land by allowing it here. Somehow its presence seemed to diminish the Biblical strength of the claim that Jews had for the land.

The time at last came when, having been without a friend to talk to for weeks, he chose to find Mirium again. On returning to Jerusalem, he took his friend out to dinner at a kosher Chinese restaurant.

"What will you have?" he asked.

"Can I have anything on the menu?" she wanted to know.

"What kind of a question is that? Of course."

"I've been away from America too long," she said. "Red meat is very expensive in Israel. I've eaten nothing but chicken and fish ever since arriving here. I'd kill for a good steak."

"Done," he said. "Waiter, your finest steak for the lady."

"What happened at Sinai?" she wanted to know.

"I guess nothing. Oh, I'll never forget the magnitude of the place. I think God still lives there, but if He heard me, He didn't speak to me."

"Did you really think He would?" Mirium asked.

"Who knows. Nothing ventured, nothing gained as the cliche goes. Anyway, now I've seen the place and I'm ready to go back. I miss my son too much."

The following morning he went to a travel agency to make arrangements for the trip to Miami. Before he could be waited on however, he was accosted by the Jewish version of the Salvation Army.

Nathan Levy wanted to know if he needed a place to stay.

"I am a bit low on cash," Robinson admitted, "but that's not the only reason I'm going home."

"If you're a Jew, then Israel *is* your home. I'm from the Yeshiva Aish Ha Torah. You can have a room there for free if you'll study the Torah with us," Nate told him.

Steve had once heard that "you haven't really seen Israel until you've studied in a yeshiva," so he accepted the offer for a few days.

At the school the writer gave a synopsis of his book's thesis over lunch. His audience was large and kind in its reception of him, with a few notable exceptions. But after he was shown to his quarters, which he was to share with five other young men, an opponent to his views walked into the room, sniffed the air as if to indicate some foul odor being present, and then stated: "I think I smell a goy." It was not the kind of greeting that the idealist was accustomed to getting. Nate told him to ignore it, but he couldn't.

By the following morning, word of the controversial author had reached the head rabbi before class began. The topic for the day was miracles. Those that were attributed to Jesus were discussed as were those which were attributed to another "false messiah," Sabbatai Sevi.

Reb Noach Weinberg pointed out that, "if a prophet predicted the sun would be blotted out the following day at 12:00 noon, and it was in fact blotted out at 12:01 P.M., the prophet was a false prophet because he had missed by one minute. That which is spoken in God's name must *all* come true. Jesus is credited with some good predictions in the New Testament, but he is also credited with a number of bad ones, such as his frequent prophecies of a quick return; indeed, one that was to occur during the lifetimes of some who were alive then."

Steve asked him how it was that Jesus could perform any miracles at all. The Reb's answer took him by surprise, for he had been devoid of mystical knowledge until that day.

"Jesus," the Reb stated confidently, "was a master of the secret Jewish art of Kabbalah. He received his power to use God's name when he sneaked into the Temple and copied the name that no man could memorize. After copying it, which was forbidden, he put it into a cut in his foot and then walked out from the Temple undetected. The Name gave him the power. Sabbatai Sevi was another Master of the Name. With it, he too was able to raise the dead and draw wine from walls."

Steve was in shock. How was it that he had heard none of this in years of research back in America? And who was this Sabbatai Sevi? Oh yes, he had heard of Sabbatai before. The man was a false Messiah that lived between 1626 and 1676. He converted to Islam. Steve never thought it worth pursuing any further information about the man after he had heard of Sevi's apostasy. But now he was asked to believe that false prophets *did* have the power to raise the dead! And through what? Kabbalah? The implications of this new data, if true, were overwhelming. For one thing, it meant that his book was instantly obsolete because it left the topic of mysticism completely out. To hear a top rabbi also credit Sabbatai with such feats also meant that Steve was going to have to do his homework again about the Turkish Jew.

Still awed by what he had heard that day, he decided to take a walk through the streets of West Jerusalem. It wasn't long before he saw a book in the window of a book shop that offered answers to many of his questions.

Sabbatai Sevi, The Mystical Messiah by Gershom Scholem, was a thousand-page masterpiece that included every single detail scholars had ever managed to dig up on the man. Robinson bought it and a few other books on Kabbalah. He returned to the yeshiva and began to study. What he learned was most unsettling.

Steve had always known and used his first Hebrew name Ithamar, though at times he had, as on the cover of his first book, misspelled it as Etomar. But on checking his circumcision certificate he learned that his full Hebrew name was Ithamar Sabbatai. He shared a common name with the apostate. This he thought was an odd coincidence, especially because he too had a certain attraction to Islam.

The book on Sevi was so long that he decided to hold

off reading it all until his return to Miami. In the meantime, he chose to concentrate on Kabbalah.

The texts made it clear that one should not attempt the study of Kabbalah until the age of forty, an idea that he quickly put aside. He read, however, of four who studied it. One died, one went crazy, one apostatized and only one, Rabbi Akiba, survived with his wits intact. There were warnings everywhere he turned. While reading on a bus to Tel Aviv one day he was again cautioned by a stranger sitting next to him.

"You're too young for that!" the man advised.

"I'm nearly thirty-one. I want to know what everybody's so afraid of," Steve told him.

"Suit yourself, friend. But I know what I'm talking about," the man replied.

He read something about a Jewish Trinity: "the Holy Ancient One, Blessed Be He," was a male part; the Shechina or female Presence of God was a second part; and then there was a Son, Adam Kadmon, the archetype man. Now he understood the warning about apostasy as a possible consequence of Kabbalistic studies. He had sacrificed a wife and son to publish a book attacking the Christian concept of the Trinity only to now read in Israel of a Jewish one. He was depressed and confused for he had gone too far too fast. Dejected, he stopped in a shop to pick up a postcard to write Carmen that perhaps he had been wrong to attack her faith. He told her that he would return soon and said he hoped that she would forgive him.

The befuddled writer spent one last Sabbath in Israel. He asked a rabbi if there was a Conservative synagogue in town. The rabbi told him that, "In Jerusalem there is one

Reform synagogue, one Conservative synagogue and 40,000 toilets."

He informed the rabbi that he'd soon return to America to be with his son. The rabbi responded: "Why? He's a goy. Forget about him!" These remarks by a "rabbi" who had so little understanding of Israel's charge to be "a light unto the nations" did little to further Steve's already shaken view of Judaism.

Steve returned to the travel agent to arrange for a scenic trip home. The first leg took him by a fancy car ferry through the Greek Islands to Pireas and Athens. He then took a week to work his way through Europe by train.

The traveler enjoyed touring Munich but was strangely hit with a feeling of terror when he got off the train in Hamburg. As he walked around the station, he seemed to "remember" being there during the Holocaust. He knew that was silly because he wasn't even born then and yet flashes of memory seemed to dance about in his mind. They were so real that he never left the station to tour the city. Instead, he took the first train out. It happened to be going to Paris, but he didn't care what the destination was. He just wanted to get far away from the place.

From Paris he went to London, then flew home.

— 2 —
A MYSTICAL RETURN

At the airport in Miami, Steve called his estranged wife to ask if she could pick him up. He had been gone for about six weeks and had returned something of a new person.

"I got your child support payments and the postcard," she told him, then added, "but I still don't want to see you, not now anyway. My mother will pick you up."

"Did you rent the house out while I was gone?" he asked.

"No."

"Then the mortgage is two months behind."

"That's your problem. You can move back into the house if you pay the present and back payments," she told him.

"I won't have my job back till the fall."

"That's your problem, too. I want you to sell the house when you can and give me the money for a settlement," she insisted.

"OK. I'll rent out some rooms for now. We'll talk more about all this later."

In the car Steve told Theresa of his experiences in Israel

and of the confusing kabbalistic material. "Maybe I might convert to Christianity now if that will get Carmen back," he mused aloud.

"That's marvelous," Theresa said with a huge smile. "But I must tell you that I can't make any promises for Carmen."

There were some things that Carmen wanted to get out of the house before she let him back in, so Theresa asked if he minded staying at a hotel for a day.

"I'm flat broke," he told her.

Theresa then loaned him one hundred dollars.

Steve's greatest desire was to see his son. His main interest in getting his wife back was in fact to have his son at home again. It was true that he still loved Carmen, and he'd yet to sleep with another in the five months of separation that had now passed. But he knew that he could always find a new romance if he'd try hard enough. Bobby, however, couldn't be replaced, so he was delighted when Theresa told him that Carmen would let him have overnight visitation, something he hadn't previously enjoyed, after he moved back to the house.

The man checked into a motel on Miami Beach and waited for the "all clear" from Carmen.

The following morning Steve took a stroll down Collins Avenue. The air was laden with scents of sea, palm and flowers as he shut his eyes to ponder the wisdom of a conversion, praying for guidance. Then he opened his eyes, walked a few more steps and saw His answer. There, before him in a newspaper box, was a paper with the word TRAITOR in bold print on page one. This time he refused to even consider looking for a scientific explanation for what he saw. Nor would he entertain any thoughts of coincidence. The answer to all his questions was before him. Ithamar Sabbatai would not become another Sabbatai Sevi. Steve would remain a Jew. If Carmen were to come back to him, it wouldn't be by way of the Church, or the Mosque, but by the chupah (marriage canopy) of a synagogue or not at all. He silently thanked God for speaking to him, then added: "Dear God, while I have Your ear, would You mind letting me know how I can get my son back again?" This time there was no immediate answer.

Steve moved back into the house the next day. He placed an ad in the *Herald* to find a roommate, registered as a substitute teacher, landed a summer job as a lifeguard, and then phoned Carmen to ask her for a date.

"I told you I'm not ready to see you," she said.

"Look, honey, it's been five months. If not now, then when?"

"When I'm ready, and not before. I may never be ready. Did you convert yet?" she wanted to know.

"No, I've decided against that. If we do get back together, I'll have to insist that you convert to Judaism. I won't confuse you with Islam again," he said.

"What happened to your new understanding of Christianity?" she asked. He told her of his prayer and its answer, knowing she'd never go along with what he was asking, then brought up the property settlement. Robert Finnerty, best man at the Robinson wedding, wanted to buy Carmen's share of the home's equity. He was willing to pay her five thousand dollars for it, which was more than fair market value.

Her attitude quickly grew colder as he told her of his

desire to hold on to his half of the house for a year, then sell it and use his part of the equity to buy a sailboat to live on.

"You'll never change," she said with an air of bitterness. "You'll always be a dreamer. That's why I could never live with you again."

"You can divorce me if you want; I can't stop it legally. We both know that," Steve replied. "But, I'm still Bobby's father. Bobby and I both deserve better visitation than we've been getting."

"You can have him for one day per week. Saturday morning at nine to Sunday at the same time," she reluctantly told him.

Bobby arrived right on time for the first of his weekly visits. Steve cherished every hour of each; indeed he soon came to measure time by how many hours were left on each visit and how many days it would be to the next. Like so many other weekend fathers, he'd always strive to make each visit more fun than the last.

The father thought he understood some of the dangers of Kabbalah by now. Still, as a science teacher, he couldn't let go of the idea that there might be some way to perform magic by the use of certain divine names. A scientist, he thought, must investigate everything, and so he read on.

The book on Sabbatai Sevi had a compelling grip on his mind. He learned that Sevi had, after his conversion, continued to practice the laws of Judaism along with the laws of Islam. This Steve had also done for about two years.

Sabbatai's conversion had occurred in Constantinople (now known as Istanbul), a place that Steve had on occasion seen in his dreams in a most troubling way . . . always in conjunction with a disaster of some sort.

Sabbatai had a scar on his private parts from a burn that he believed had a supernatural origin when he was six years old. Steve had a scar in the same place of unexplained origin. And it was Sabbatai's third marriage that was most successful. Steve could only hope that the same would prove true for him, too, for Carmen had not been his first wife. His original mate had been an intelligent but overly domineering and talkative Jewish girl from New York who had once nagged him into going to podiatry school for a year. They had been through a "friendly divorce" five years before. There were no children from the marriage.

None of the Sabbatai business would have seized on his imagination if it hadn't been for the common Hebrew name that the two shared. The book on the Turk also mentioned that early Sevi followers believed their hero would reincarnate. When another false Messiah arose in the next century, a man by the name of Jacob Frank (1726-1791), he too converted (to Catholicism) but not before stating that he thought he was "the gilgol" (reincarnation) of Sabbatai Sevi. Steve was becoming more intrigued with each passing page of Scholem's book.

One night while his son was staying over, the aspiring mystic attempted to meditate on the divine names of the Sephirot on the Kabbalistic Tree of Life. He had been watching a Phillies-Pirates baseball game and had just turned it off. Bobby was in bed next to him, asleep, as the man started to focus the Hebrew letters of the esoteric "ladder to heaven" in his mind. Soon he too was asleep. Suddenly the father was awakened by a scream of horror from Bobby. All was dark but he could hear that the toddler, now well over two, had gone downstairs. The boy had never done this before at night.

Steve rushed below to find his son in a state of terror in the dining room. Normally Bobby was very talkative. But on this night he was unable to find words to let his father know what had frightened him so. It took nearly a half hour to stop his tears which was also highly unusual. Bobby generally only cried when it was time to return to his mother (which is not to say that he didn't love his mother, but that the boy didn't want to be without his father). At last, feeling secure once again, he fell asleep on his dad's chest as Steve carried him upstairs to go back to bed.

The morning brought with it a scene right out of Amityville Horror, for wherever Steve had lain the night before, there lay a pool of blood marking the spot. He checked his chest for cuts. There were none. At first glance it looked like the blood had oozed through his skin at the level of his heart. Steve searched his body desperately for bruises that might give a natural explanation for what he was finding, but still there were none. He thought that he might have had a nosebleed though he had never had one before, but there wasn't a drop of blood to be found anywhere on his face. What was even stranger was that none of the blood which lay on the sheets had clung to his body. The stuff was all over his bed, but nowhere on his person. Was this the result of his kabbalistic meditation? Could it be so easy to gain a hot line to the Almighty? Yes, he had seen many signs before that had given him the impression that Someone upstairs knew and cared about him, but nothing so dramatic as this. He was awed by the experience, but terrified as well. What was God trying to tell him? Whatever it was, it didn't look like a friendly greeting to be sure.

Still upset, he drove Bobby back to his mother's, returned home, and called a Lubavitcher rabbi for an opinion. The rabbi *knew* instantly what the novice had done wrong.

"You have taken the name of the Lord in vain!" he asserted.

"What can I do about it?" Steve anxiously asked.

"Take whatever books you're using out to a Jewish cemetery and bury them there. They can't be thrown out because they contain the divine names. You must dispose of them as we would any old prayer book," the rabbi said.

Steve wasn't too happy about disposing of all the books he had acquired dealing with Kabbalah. Instead he chose to wait another day before making a decision. That night he slept downstairs on the sofa.

When he awoke the next morning, the sofa was covered with blood. Now he was really scared. He ran to a neighbor to borrow a shovel and was about to head for the nearest Jewish cemetery when he finally calmed down and decided to apply the scientific method to investigate the phenomena.

The first step, he knew, was to understand the problem. The problem, he hoped, was not that God was punishing him, but that there was blood of an unexplained origin on the bedding. He went upstairs and stretched out on the mattress. At first it did appear as if the blood was from the level of the heart. But then when he curled up as he knew he usually did while asleep, he saw that the blood was in fact from the area of his nose. There was also a heavy concentration on the pillows, and he usually slept with them over his eyes to keep out the morning light. He hypothesized the cause to be a nosebleed, probably psychosomatically induced, which he had wiped off on the pillows or blankets as he slept. As for what had terrified his son, the boy usually slept snuggled up under his father's arm, but on that night Steve had fallen asleep on the other side of the king-sized bed. Bobby might have woken up, not felt his father, and then gone downstairs to look for him. Finding nothing but blackness below, the boy panicked thinking that his father had abandoned him. It all seemed to make sense now although he still felt that a nosebleed should have left some trace of blood on his face. He went back to reading about Kabbalah.

A month later the man found that he had a new medical problem to deal with. He had injured his neck, and it had swollen painfully on the right side. A chiropractor had been treating it with manual adjustments and with acupuncture, but the swelling hadn't really gone down by much. Steve was aware that his neck had always been a bit swollen even before the injury. He wanted an M.D. to see it.

The chiropractor hadn't told Steve because he didn't want to alarm him, but he initially suspected Hodgkins disease, a form of cancer that used to be nearly always fatal. It had, however, been found that by cutting out the spleen there was an eighty percent recovery rate, but the man had been determined to cure his patient's problems through acupuncture. He was a bit upset when Steve let him know that he was going to see Doctor Katz, a surgeon that his health plan had referred him to.

A nurse took Steve's blood pressure before Dr. Katz came in to examine him. It was a bit high, 139 over 95. Normally his pressure had run at or slightly below normal, but the stress of the times had caught up with him.

When the surgeon walked in, he took the history and placed both hands on his patient's neck to feel what the problem was.Then he mumbled something about being impressed.

Robinson asked him what he thought it was. The doctor told him first what he thought it wasn't.

"It doesn't feel like Hodgkins," he said as Steve heaved a sigh of relief, "and it doesn't feel like just a pulled muscle or a spinal injury."

Concerned that something might have grown in his neck, Steve asked what the chances were that it was some form of cancer. He expected an immediate "zero" from the doctor. He didn't get it.

"Oh, about fifty-fifty," the doctor said.

Steve nearly passed out. They had to catch him and lay him back. His blood pressure dropped instantly with the news to ninety over sixty. After fifteen minutes, it climbed back towards normal, and the doctor ordered him into Cedars of Lebanon Hospital for some tests later that day.

At Cedars the good news was that the growth was likely a giant nonmalignant cyst. Doctor Katz explained the options. "If we lance it, we can drain it but it will certainly fill up again. You'd have to repeat the procedure every few months for the rest of your life. Then again, while I don't think it's cancer, there is always a slight chance that it is. If it were cancer, then lancing the area would allow malignant cells to be spread to the rest of your body. If it were my neck, I'd cut it out," he advised.

What kind of a scar will it leave?" Steve wanted to know.

"Expect a fine white line about three inches long,"

Katz said.

Surgery was scheduled for early the next day. It was just a cyst, about the size of a grapefruit.

Back in his room the next day, Steve read more of his book on Sabbatai Sevi. It seems that Sevi's apostasy had occurred after he had been arrested by the Sultan of Turkey. The Sultan had heard that Sabbatai was believed by many to have been the Messiah, and the head Turk was anxious to avoid making the mistake of Pontius Pilate. Although Sabbatai had been placed under arrest, it was in a prison that looked more like a palace than a dungeon. There was gold and silver everywhere. The walls were lined with regal carpets.

When Sabbatai was finally summoned before the Sultan, he was asked to perform a miracle. Unfortunately, his supernatural feats had all been the production of "rumor mills." There was no substance to any of them. The result was disaster. The Sultan gave him a simple choice: he could become a Muslim or he could have his head cut off.

It was a black time for the Jews of Europe. The rabbis had predicted that a holocaust would befall the Jewish people just before Israel was to be restored. In 1648 a holocaust of huge proportions had occurred. Ever since Poland's annexation of the Ukraine in 1569, Jews had been working with the Polish government to administer the conquered territories. The Catholic Church also had a need for tax collectors who would gather in funds from the Ukrainian Eastern Orthodox Churches of Poland. Who could be better to choose for the task than the Jews?

Cossacks were anything but thrilled about the prospects of passing on their hard-earned money to the Polish nobles or to the Catholic Church by way of the hated "Christ killers," so they revolted. Led by Bogan Chmielnicki, the Cossacks (later joined by Polish peasants) wiped out three hundred Jewish communities and killed more than 100,000 Jews. This, the remaining Jews of Europe were certain, was the anticipated premessianic tribulation.

With word of Sabbatai's miracles growing and spreading by the day in Europe, Jews were so certain their redemption was at hand that they sold their homes and businesses for half the fair market value, moved out onto the streets and waited for a heavenly trumpet and a magical cloud to cart them off to Palestine. Of course, none arrived. What did greet the expectant Jews of Europe was the double blow that: 1) Sabbatai was not the Messiah and 2) he had thought it more important to save his head than to save his religion. The Jews could have accepted the death of their Messiah, as had those who had followed Jesus. But for most, apostasy was another matter. Sabbatai would have been better off, Steve felt, by letting the sword fall upon his neck.

The scar that grew on Ithamar Sabbatai's neck after he left the hospital was a far cry from the promised thin white line. Instead, it was long, thick and ugly. Kids would tell him that it looked as if someone had tried to cut his head off. Everywhere he went people would ask him about what had happened. After a while the questions grew so annoying that he decided to have plastic surgery done to reduce it. The scar came back again, though not as bad as it was before. Each time he thought about Sabbatai Sevi's apostasy, he felt that the scar on his own neck should have been on Sevi's instead. Perhaps, he sometimes suspected, it was part of his "tiqqun" or payment for mistakes that he had made in a previous life, a life where he had been known as Sabbatai Sevi. This belief, which would grow as fate began to throw at Steve a relentless series of coincidental similarities with the Turk, would one day be seen by Carmen and a future attorney as a reason to keep the boy from his father.

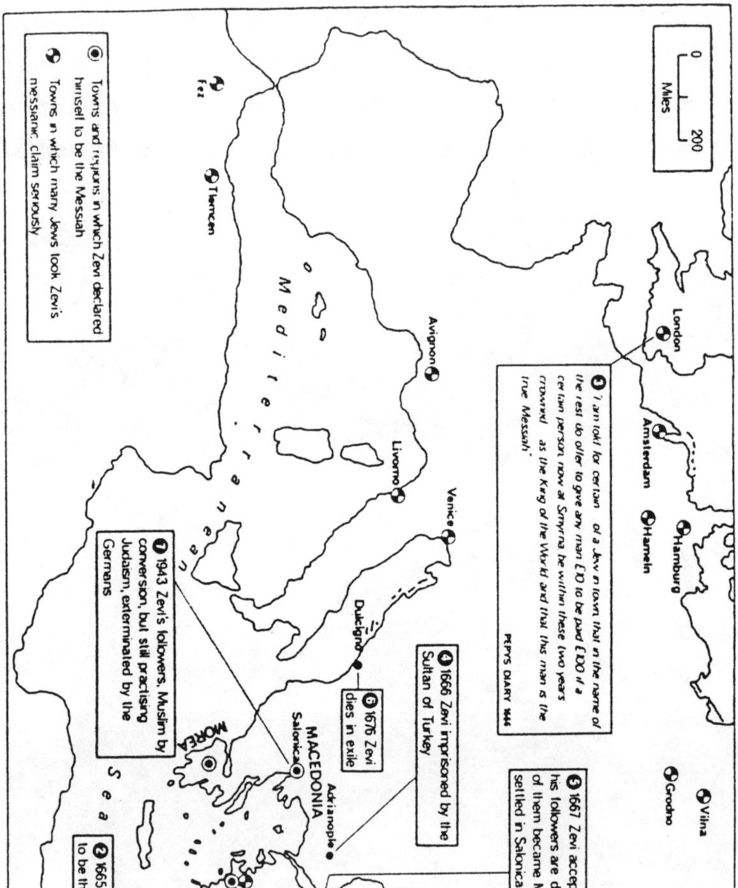
SABBATAI ZEVI
1626-1676
0 Miles 200
London
Amsterdam
Hamburg
Hameln
Vilna
Grodno
Avignon
Livorno
Venice
Dulcigno
Salonica
MACEDONIA
MOREA
Adrianople
Constantinople
Smyrna
Aleppo
SYRIA
Jerusalem
Gaza
EGYPT
Cairo
Fez
Tlemcen
Mediterranean Sea
1626 Zevi born
1665 Zevi declares himself to be the Messiah
"I am told for certain of a Jew in town that in the name of the rest do offer to give any man £10 to be paid £100 if a certain person now at Smyrna be within these two years as the King of the World and that this man is the true Messiah."
PEPYS DIARY 1666
1666 Zevi imprisoned by the Sultan of Turkey
1667 Zevi accepts Islam. Most of his followers are disillusioned. A remnant of them became Muslims with him, and settled in Salonica
1676 Zevi dies in exile
1943 Zevi's followers, Muslim by conversion, but still practising Judaism, exterminated by the Germans
Towns and regions in which Zevi declared himself to be the Messiah
Towns in which many Jews took Zevi's messianic claim seriously

— 3 —
THE ROAD TO COURT

Carmen agreed to sell her half of the home's equity to Bob Finnerty, and Steve agreed to pay off all joint debts. He returned to his teaching job and kept trying to get his wife to date him, but to no avail. By November, eleven months after Carmen had pulled out, Steve had fallen in love with a Jewish divorcee named Diane.

The thirty-year-old was attractive, but not overly beautiful. She had great wit and Steve particularly enjoyed the fact that, unlike his wife, Diane loved a good intellectual exchange. She also had a little girl about a year older than his son. Bobby was nuts about both of them, and the four made many trips together to Disney World on weekends. By December Steve was determined to marry his new love, but there was one major problem. Carmen had done nothing to finalize the divorce.

He decided to call Carmen to ask her out one last time, knowing full well that she'd turn him down again. She did, and it was then that he began to push for the divorce.

"Look, Carmen, it's been a year now. You don't date me and you won't set me free. I've got to get on with my life. Why not set a court date and finalize things?" he asked.

"I don't want to do anything for now, but if you file I won't oppose you," she informed him.

"I don't want the divorce, but I can't go on like this. My attorney has said that so long as we stick to the property settlement agreement, all we'll need at court is a witness as to six months state residency. Will you bring your mother in for that?" he wanted to know.

"I suppose. Get a court date and call me back."

A final hearing was set for January 20, 1980. When the big day rolled around, Steve was at the courthouse early with his lawyer. All either of the two parties had to do was utter five simple words: "This marriage is irretrievably broken." It seemed so simple. Five words and he'd be free to marry again, though his love hadn't yet accepted the proposal.

As Carmen came up the steps, her husband sensed that things weren't going to go down as he'd planned. She was alone.

"Where's your mother?" he asked.

"She's not coming. I don't want the divorce today," she told him.

"Want to give our marriage another chance?" he asked nervously.

"No, let's keep things just as they are," she responded.

"Look, Carmen, I've heard you're thinking of taking a job as a stewardess. If you go in there today, you'll have custody of Bobby. But if you don't, and if you take that job so you're out of town nights on a regular basis, I'll take him from you."

"Suit yourself," she told him, then turned and walked

out of the courtroom. Totally dumbfounded by her actions, he called Theresa to see if she knew what was going on. Not only was his mother-in-law in the dark as well, but she was furious when she heard about her daughter's refusal to get it over with. A week later he learned his wife had taken the airline job and the fight was on.

Diane, in the meantime, had decided to not accept his proposal. "I enjoy being with you," she assured Steve, "but after twelve years of marital tyranny, I want to enjoy my freedom for a while." By "freedom" Diane meant sexual freedom, something that would soon lose much of its value when Herpes and then AIDS began to terrorize the singles' scene in Miami. At any rate, while Steve was heartbroken, he rationalized that it would probably be quite a while before he'd be free to marry anyway.

Robinson set out to find a new attorney with a sense of the jugular vein. The man hired was John Oskowitz, a tall, slender young Jew who looked like a shark.

Steve told him the case history and asked what his chances for success were. The attorney drew up a chart with pluses and minuses for each side, what he called the equities of the parties.

On Robinson's side was the fact that he was a college graduate, while Carmen had only a G.E.D. high school diploma. Steve was home every night; Carmen wasn't. The child seemed to have more of an affinity for his father, who was a professional educator, a published author, a county champion track coach, and a man who was actively involved in raising money for charitable organizations.

Against Steve would be the fact that Carmen would undoubtedly portray him as a religious fanatic. More, he had nobody to help him with the boy while he was at work, and the boy was "of tender years." Florida law hadn't yet advanced, and at the time, all things being equal, a child of tender years was always given to the mother. Also on Carmen's side was that she now lived with a large and caring family which included other children for Bobby to play with, and the fact that Judge Watts was, like Carmen's mother, a practicing Catholic.

John wanted to know more about the book which Steve had written. He wasn't encouraged when he learned that the work had actually attacked the Catholic Church. Nor was he happy about the prospect that Carmen would try to prove Steve had irresponsibly run off to Israel.

"Let me put it this way," John said. "You've got a good shot at custody, but there are three things working against you. One: The mother usually wins when the kid is of tender years. Two: You're Jewish. Three: You're a Jew who attacked the judge's church. Don't be discouraged, but I'd be a liar if I didn't give it to you straight. Would you settle for joint custody if I could get it?"

"You bet I would."

Steve gave him a five-hundred-dollar retainer and the name of Carmen's attorney, Frank Gomez. He wasn't yet adamant in his demand for full custody. He just wanted the divorce along with a guarantee of adequate visitation.

John phoned Gomez after Steve had gone. What he heard didn't serve to increase his optimism about the case. Gomez made it clear that the other side had a bundle to spend and he intended to milk the case for all it was worth. In short, there would be no quick agreement.

At the initial hearing, the judge ordered the Robinsons

to be seen by Henry Knolls of the Conciliation Unit. This was customary. Attorneys weren't permitted to be present, and such sessions were occasionally successful at defusing disagreements before they became overly hostile.

Steve was determined to be calm and flexible when he appeared before Knolls. After more than a year of lousy visitation, he had little to lose. Carmen, however, was nervous, angry and hostile as she approached the sessions. She even refused to show up at all for the first two appointments. Steve didn't mind her intransigence. He knew it would be in Knolls' report, and he needed all the help he could get.

When Carmen finally did show up, she wasted no time at all before stating her opposition to conciliation. "My husband is insane and a dangerous influence on my child," she asserted.

"The court is unlikely to deny visitation if that's what you want," Knolls told her.

"If that's so, then the madman shouldn't be allowed more than one or two nights per week," she smugly remarked.

Knolls told her, a bit sarcastically, "I don't understand. If you think your husband's crazy, why would you allow him to see the boy at all?"

"I don't want him to have visitation rights, but if the court must order it, I want it kept to a minimum. The man belongs in a padded cell. He thinks he's a prophet," she asserted.

"You're the one who's nuts!" Steve angrily shouted at her. "I never thought of myself that way!" It was, of course, true that Steve talked to God at times. But he never heard voices or claimed to speak for the Lord. And when he did talk to God, it was only when he thought nobody was around to hear him. The conversations, he knew, were one way. Sometimes there might be things that he interpreted as "signs" but that was a long way from claiming to be a Moses, even if he did go to Sinai to make his prayers heard.

Carmen went on to tell Knolls that she feared Steve would poison Bobby's mind about Christianity by telling the boy about what the Nazis did to the Jews. She pointed out that Steve had often mentioned the Concordat between the Vatican and the Nazi government. Her mother told her that he had even written about it in his book.

When the mediator heard how she phrased her concern, he was surprised. "Mrs. Robinson," he asked, "haven't you yourself read the book? Your husband told me that it had, in fact, been dedicated to you as well as Bobby!"

"The topic bores me. I don't need to read it. I've heard it all a thousand times before from my husband. He had a one-track mind and never shut up about the damn thing."

Knolls pushed hard for an agreement and almost succeeded that day. Steve was willing to give her custody so long as his weekend visitation periods started on Friday. Carmen was willing to give him Saturday to Monday mornings. The father wanted to have his son on board an Irwin 37 sloop that he and Bob Finnerty hoped to buy for extended weekend charters to the Bahamas. He couldn't wait until Saturday morning to sail. The two would never come so close to an out-of-court agreement again.

Steve had filed for custody back in February, 1980. The divorce and custody hearing was set for September of the same year. The interim period was filled with motions, petitions and counter-petitions of every possible nature. The legal road to court was like an obstacle course, and at times Steve wondered if he'd ever get to the finish line. Carmen's attorney challenged the sale of her interest in the house to Finnerty, and another buyer sued Robinson and Finnerty for not having clear title to the property. Legal costs ate up any possibility of closing a deal on the boat.

Carmen's attorney asked the judge to order psychological evaluations of all the parties concerned. He had hoped to prove Steve insane, but his efforts backfired. Steve, fully in control of his faculties and well versed on all the tests thrown at him due to his own psychology degree, was able to come out of the evaluation with a much stronger case.

As she did with the mediator, Carmen again failed to keep two appointments at the psychologist's office. When she finally did arrive, unfamiliar with the battery of tests thrown at her, she distorted the truth about several items, was caught repeatedly, and wound up leaving the psychologist with a very negative impression.

Bobby's love for his father dominated the boy's session with Dr. Elinson. He was also full of comments about fearing Mommy who hit him a lot. Every other word out of his mouth was about how he wanted to live with his father, which was most impressive because it was his mother who took him there. In the end the doctor wrote a report to the court identifying Steve as the primary psychological parent and recommending that he be given full custody.

The court also ordered an H.R.S. social worker to do a home study. Steve had been living in a Miami Beach hotel ever since he had sold his furniture prior to the thwarted purchase of the boat that he hoped to live on. He couldn't very well be interviewed there, so he rented a large and beautifully furnished home in Kendall a day before Martha Anderson came around to visit him. When Martha arrived, Bobby was playing in an ideal child's room with his one-hour-old electric train set. Around the boy was an impressive children's library and an abundance of toys. Steve had every moment masterfully planned. He showed her how well he had taught Bobby to swim and dive, and he also did a good job telling about all the fights he had to endure to get access to his son.

"My main concern is that Bobby grow up to love both parents," he told her.

By the time Martha arrived at Carmen's home, Bobby was well aware of what was at stake. The lad recognized her at the door, ran right up and told her straight away in front of Carmen and her mother, "Tell Mommy what I told you before. I wanna live with my Daddy. Ask Mommy if I can be with Daddy."

Carmen argued, "As you can see, Bobby's been brainwashed by his father. I think it's best that the man be kept from my son completely so this won't happen again." Martha's report, therefore, concluded as did Dr. Elinson's, that while the father would encourage a loving relationship with the mother if he were awarded custody, the mother by contrast would harm the boy psychologically if she won by doing all in her power to keep him from his father. It was also pointed out that Bobby appeared to love his dad and identify with him the most anyway.

Anderson's report was not entirely negative about Carmen. "In the mother's favor is that she is willing to teach her son about his Jewish heritage. Mr. Robinson, on the other hand, will not consent to have his son attend church as well as synagogue. He does not accept the divinity of Jesus and believes it to be a violation of basic Jewish doctrine to worship him." Martha, a Protestant, could understand some of his criticisms of the Catholic Church, but she felt he was a bit too inflexible about joint religious exposure. Still, overall she had no difficulty in recommending to Judge Watts that Steve be granted full custody. The dual expert witness recommendations in Steve's favor were important victories, and Steve felt sure that his prayer on Sinai was about to be answered. John, however, reminded him that Watts was Catholic. "You know," he said, "I don't know that the man will show any prejudice with respect to religion, but I can't over-emphasize that no matter how good a case we appear to have, Bobby is still of tender years. You've got to overcome that issue and the fact that you don't have any help in raising the boy."

Steve hoped that John was just covering himself. He knew the issues, but could not seriously imagine that any judge would ever ignore the weight of all expert testimony.

— 4 —
BEFORE JUDGE WATTS

A full day had been allocated for the trial with Steve's witnesses appearing in the morning and Carmen's in the afternoon. In the father's corner were his attorney, Dr. Elinson, Martha Anderson, Dr. Garnet (principal at Steve's school), a fellow teacher, and Steve's mother. With Carmen were her lawyer, her brothers and her mother as well as a friend of the family who had been present on a day just after the separation had begun when Steve had tried to take Bobby from Theresa's house only to wind up at the police station. He remembered her from the scene twenty months earlier because the woman had called him a "Kike."

Robinson was so nervous that he hadn't slept a wink all the night before. By now he had developed a nervous tic on his thigh to complement the one on his eye. He didn't think he could take much more aggravation. Each trip to Theresa's house to pick up his son for visitation had been fraught with danger. There was never a guarantee that his wife would get the boy there on time; and when she didn't, which was a frequent problem, he'd get so upset that he'd create a scene. Inevitably her older brothers would come out, and

Steve would get into a fist fight with them on the lawn.

Although Steve's mother was aware of her son's grief, she had mixed emotions about testifying against Carmen. For one thing, she liked her daughter-in-law. Carmen had been, in her mind, a good mother to Bobby. She had even given Steve's mother special visitation with Bobby when Steve wasn't around. Anxious about being placed in a position that would require her to testify against a woman that she sympathized with, she told her son that if she didn't get called to testify by that afternoon, she wouldn't return to do so on another day.

"Call her as a witness only after we've exhausted all other favorable testimony," John advised his client. "Anyway," he continued, "the judge will assume that she'll testify in your behalf. It might be better to let him go on thinking that way. Gomez might use her more for his purposes than ours. Jesus, doesn't she care that Bobby will grow up Christian if you lose?"

"Mom's not very religious. She said I should have known what I was getting into when I married Carmen in the first place."

Judge Watts then entered. He was a stout little man with the face of a bulldog. He had a bored look about him as if to say he had heard it all before. This was Robinson's first look at him, and he didn't like what he saw. There was a certain lack of compassion that the man exuded.

After the initial opening formalities were over, John began with a statement of Steve's position:

"Your honor, twenty-one months ago my client's wife removed herself from the marital residence, taking the child with her. In January of this year, both parties came to the courthouse to terminate the marriage after a property settlement agreement had been reached. Mrs. Robinson, however, refused to go through with the divorce on that day and she also rejected taking any action which might save the marriage, be it moving back in with my client, dating him or attending any counseling sessions for which he was willing to pay. When the property settlement was signed, my client was willing to yield custody of the minor child of his marriage to Mrs. Robinson. Since that time there has been a substantial change of circumstances, to wit: Mrs. Robinson has since taken a job as a flight attendant with Northwest Orient Airlines. She is frequently out of town, often overnighting in Seoul or Seattle. The minor child is thus left without a caring parent for up to three or four days per week.

"By contrast, Mr. Robinson is a professional educator who is home each afternoon. If my client is granted custody, he intends to place the child in a nursery school during the day while he works, and then pick up the boy, Bobby, each afternoon after work. Further, as you requested in an earlier pretrial hearing, all parties involved have been tested by Dr. Elinson, and interviewed by Mrs. Anderson, an H.R.S. social worker. Both of these expert witnesses will testify that Mr. Robinson is the primary psychological parent and both will state that it is their belief the father, Mr. Robinson, should be granted sole custody of the child."

Having finished his summary, John sat down.

Gomez was on next. Speaking with a strong Cuban accent, he began:

"Your honor, Mrs. Robinson has taken a job as a flight

attendant because it best allows her to support herself and the child. Her job is a respectful one which pays far more than most jobs do for high school graduates. Further, although she is occasionally out of town overnight, the child is left in the loving care of his grandmother. Mrs. Robinson not only lives now with her mother, but with a large family that includes several children for Bobby to play with. By contrast, Mr. Robinson is quite alone and without any assistance at all when it comes to raising this child. We will show that the home Bobby is now living in is a happy family situation. The child is well cared for there. As for the reports of the so-called expert witnesses, we will show that Mr. Robinson's psychology degree gave him an unfair advantage over my client. He knew about many of the tests in advance. Further, it appears that he brainwashed the child into misbehaving when Mrs. Anderson came to visit his mother. More than these things, we will show your honor that Robinson is a religious fanatic who is bent on the destruction of the Christian religion, a man who must be denied access to the child so that the boy will be spared from possible psychological damage that his father may cause. Already the father has alienated the affections of the child towards his mother. We will ask your honor to put a stop to this."

At this time John called Elinson, who was first asked about his credentials which included a Bachelors and a Masters degree from Princeton University and a Ph.D. from Columbia, all in clinical psychology. The doctor had practiced in Miami for ten years and was often called in by the Court for custody cases.

John interrogated him about when he had seen the parties and then began the serious questioning:

"Can you tell us about some of the tests you performed?"

"With Mr. Robinson, I administered a battery of tests which included Human-figure drawings, the Bender Gestalt, the Elinson Projective Sentence Completion Test, the Minnesota Multiphasic Personality Inventory, and the Thematic Apperception Test. Mrs. Robinson took the same battery. She has also provided me with several letters that her husband has written since the divorce proceedings were initiated. My file also includes a social investigation completed by Martha Anderson of H.R.S. In the case of the little boy, Robert, I had him make several free drawings, and I gave him the Peabody Picture Vocabulary Test, the Rorshach, the Elinson Children's Incomplete Sentence Test and the Thematic Apperception Test. I also had access to all of the child's health records including a neurological evaluation by Dr. Robert Cohen dated July 11, 1980. My opinions are based on evaluation of all data just cited."

John then asked him what he had been able to learn of Mr. Robinson's background. Elinson replied:

"Mr. Robinson was born in Philadelphia, Pennsylvania. He has resided in Dade County for the past seven years. He has a Bachelor of Arts degree in psychology from the University of Pennsylvania, but he now possesses twice as many general science credits as he does in his degree field. The man is employed as a science teacher and track coach by the Dade County School Board with a placement at Killian Senior High. In addition, Mr. Robinson teaches at a Hebrew school, Beth David. He also has authored and recently published a book entitled *The Great Christ Debate.*"

John asked him whether or not Steve had told him why he was seeking custody. Elinson replied:

"He said that he thinks he can better provide for Robert's physical and emotional needs. Mr. Robinson also feels that he can provide his son with a better academic and religious education, a stable and consistent living situation and a strong parent-child relationship."

"Did Mr. Robinson relate any fears about leaving Bobby in his mother's care?" John asked.

"Very definitely. Mr. Robinson gave a lengthy and consistent account of his troubled relationship with his wife. He alleged that his wife did not want to have the child and that she suffered from postpartum depression after Robert was born. He also felt that she became more self-conscious of her physical appearance after Bobby was born via a Caesarean section."

With that, Steve's mind flashed back to just how lovely Carmen had been before the operation. He could see her dancing before him in a motel in Norfolk while he was in the Navy. She wore a see-through, orange night gown. He loved to look at her abdomen in those days. In fact, it was one of the most exquisitely perfect forms that his eyes had ever been privileged to behold, and he had later cursed the doctor who had butchered "God's work of art."

"Mr. Robinson," Elinson continued, "expressed concern that his wife frequently left Bobby in the care of her mother. He described this woman as a careless person who occasionally left poisons laying around the house. In discussing the relationship with his mother-in-law, it was obvious that the differences between these two are extreme and at times quite bitter."

John pressed him more by asking if there were any other serious concerns that Steve had.

"Yes," Elinson answered, "it was clear that religious issues weigh heavily in the present legal battle. Mr. Robinson is Jewish and his wife was raised as a Christian. He described himself as a traditional and Conservative Jew. He said that he wanted his wife to convert to his faith, but that her mother strongly opposed this. Apparently there have been many extended family debates and disputes about religious teaching and dogma. He showed me a certificate to prove that his son was circumcised and provided with a Jewish mohel after birth. He claims that his mother-in-law made demands that the child be baptized Catholic."

"Is this the circumcision certificate that Mr. Robinson showed you?" John asked.

"It is," Elinson replied,

"Let the record so reflect. Your honor, we would like to admit a copy of the certificate as our Exhibit A," John said.

Watts asked Gomez if he had any objections. Gomez did not. John continued with his questioning by asking Elinson to describe the nature of Steve's relationship with Bobby.

"There's obviously a great deal of affection between these two. Mr. Robinson told me that Bobby was 'his whole life.' Bobby likewise sees his father as almost a godlike figure. Throughout the course of the interview, Mr. Robinson impressed me as a conscientious and concerned parent whose motivation for seeking custody at this time is based on a concern for his son's physical, emotional and spiritual well-being."

John asked if Elinson saw Steve as being a vengeful person. The doctor said that Steve had often bent over backwards to try to reach an accommodation with his wife. He pointed out that during mediation the father had offered to yield custody in exchange for liberal visitation. Watts remarked that he saw that in Mr. Knoll's report.

John next asked Dr. Elinson if he saw Steve as a religious fanatic.

"Not at all," the doctor answered, "At one point the man even considered converting to Christianity in an effort to save his marriage, but he later decided that such an action would not be appropriate. The only thing extreme about this man is his devotion to his son."

Oskowitz then inquired about Steve's intellectual ability and his present mental state.

"Formal psychological evaluation," Elinson replied, "reveals Mr. Robinson to be of superior intellectual ability. There was no evidence of major mental disturbance or serious psychopathology elicited during either the testing phase or the interview phase of my study concerning the man. All indications are that Mr. Robinson approached the test situation with a normal degree of defensiveness. He's an outgoing person who's basically optimistic in terms of his approach to life. He is likely to display good-humored euphoria for the most part, but on occasion he can become irritable with outbursts of anger and over activity with emotional excitement. Mr. Robinson is a very social person who can be quite extroverted, poised, and confident in social and group situations. His social adjustment is quite adequate, and he's able to tolerate demanding and challenging work situations."

John asked him how he had arrived at that conclusion, and Elinson proceeded to cite a number of sentence completion answers that Steve had given. The last question Steve had been given was one about what three wishes he would ask for if he knew that they could be magically granted. He listed, in order, Peace on Earth, custody of his son, and better knowledge of God along with more strength in trying to keep His laws. Steve's answers had convinced Elinson that he was a highly principled and caring parent who would dedicate substantial time and effort toward child rearing. Elinson stated that the man had the stamina it took to be an effective single parent.

John next questioned Elinson about Carmen.

"Mrs. Robinson," Elinson began, "was mildly anxious and superficially cooperative. She stated at the onset that she simply wanted a divorce but she thought that her husband was trying to get even by going for custody. Her chief complaints about Mr. Robinson were related to financial difficulties that the couple were having and personality problems."

When asked if Dr. Elinson thought Carmen would encourage visitation between father and son, the doctor stated "hardly," and then went on to document her bitter attitude toward her husband. He also spoke of the fist fights that Steve had to endure to get access to Bobby.

"What exactly did your testing reveal about Carmen?" John asked.

"Mrs. Robinson possesses average intelligence. There were no major psychopathological problems or mental disturbances," he said much as he had with Steve, yet then went on to add, "but there were some personality problems. Mrs. Robinson is an active and sociable woman, however she is highly self-centered and narcissistic."

You could see a look of hatred come over Carmen's face as Elinson continued: "Others may perceive her as being impulsive, immature, and acting without sufficient forethought. Her competitiveness, persuasiveness, and social aggressiveness may cause others to see her as opportunistic and manipulative. There's also a strong tendency to deny psychological difficulties where they may exist."

Perhaps because he still cared for her, Steve felt sorry for Carmen. He actually disagreed with most of the psychologist's attack on her, especially the part about her being immature. But he was hardly in a position to protest. Anyway, he reckoned, that was what she was paying an attorney for.

Some of Carmen's sentence completion answers looked like carbon copies of Steve's. She had, in fact, read Elinson's report on her husband before walking into the psychologist's office and had probably decided that she could minimize the differences between the two by mimicking his responses. But when each was asked about their greatest weakness, Steve had known the testing procedure well enough to be honest, while she had not. He listed his big mouth as his greatest weakness while his wife answered in terms of "Bobby's big brown eyes." Her answer was cute, Elinson said, but didn't reveal a willingness to confront the fact that we all have real personality weaknesses of some sort. Steve admitted that he hated Theresa, but Carmen would only admit to hating "plastic people."

When asked what she did when Bobby misbehaved, she told Elinson that Bobby was never bad. The boy was indeed very well-behaved, but all kids do things wrong at some time, Elinson told the Court, so she had to be covering up something. A talk with Bobby revealed the truth, that she hit him frequently.

John then began to ask Elinson about Bobby himself.

"Before the evaluation," Elinson said, "I observed Bobby and his mother in the waiting room. He was sitting next to her and giving her affectionate hugs and kisses. He did, however, separate easily from her, and he appeared to enjoy the individual attention afforded by the psychological evaluation. I found him to be a pleasant, active and spontaneous child who knew my name and did understand as best a three-and-a-half-year-old can that the purpose of our visit had to do with the Mommy-and-Daddy problem. I did not question Robert directly concerning this and all information was by means of the psychological tests and techniques that I described before."

John then asked, "Mrs. Robinson expressed concern about Bobby's mental stability. Did you find any evidence of a problem in this area?"

Elinson stated: "Robert is functioning within the normal limits for a child of his age. He is in some ways socially precocious and overly concerned with the conflict between his parents. The boy is verbally articulate for his age yet his word recognition is mildly deficient. There is, to answer your question, no indication that either parent has harmed his mental stability in any way."

The attorney wanted to know what the sentence completion test had revealed, and Elinson answered by quoting Bobby:

"I like my father but . . . *I like my Mother, too.*

"My secret is . . . *My Mommy takes me to the zoo and beach but my Daddy takes me to Monkey Jungle and other good places, too.*

"When I get mad . . . *I cry and my Mommy hits me.*

"When I get sad . . . *I cry and Mommy hits me.*

"My three wishes are . . . (1) *Have a birdie.* (2) *That I can go to sleep and there are no ghosts.* (3) *Be with my Daddy.*"

Elinson said that he asked Bobby about the last wish and Bobby said, "My Mommy don't take care of me but my Daddy does. So Daddy is better." Again Elinson pointed out that he asked the boy to explain what he meant. Bobby told him, "Mommy's never home when she's supposed to be. Daddy do more things with me."

"What about the other tests?" John asked.

Elinson said, "On the apperception test I showed a picture of two parents fighting. Bobby told the story as follows: '*A Daddy and a Mommy are fighting. Daddy wins. He is bigger and stronger. I love him very much.*' Another picture showed a man and a woman pulling on a child. Bobby gave this description: '*Daddy was going to get Bobby — Daddy won — Mommy didn't won Bobby.*' In a later scene which depicts a woman crying and a man walking out the door with a suitcase, Bobby says: '*Mommy is crying and Daddy won. Daddy is going back because he is the best. It's going to be over — the problem. I want Daddy to win.*' As my report indicates, there were a large number of such responses."

John inquired what it all meant, and Elinson stated, "My overall impression is that we're dealing with a child who is extremely perceptive of the present parental conflict. He appears to be most strongly identified with his father as the primary psychological parent. Bobby does express positive feelings towards both parental figures, and both parental figures are seen as significant sources of nurturance and affection."

John then pushed for the clincher by asking Elinson if he could make a recommendation for custody. Elinson didn't hesitate:

"The information I have compiled leads without doubt to the conclusion that Bobby's best interest would lie in a placement with his father as the custodial parent. I base my opinion on the fact that Mr. Robinson is the primary psychological parent as far as Bobby is concerned, and that his needs could most closely be attended by his father. I also feel that Mr. Robinson would encourage and support Bobby's visitation with his mother, whereas I feel that Mrs. Robinson would strive to keep contact with the noncustodial parent at a minimum. I would like to add that the poor communication which exists between Mr. and Mrs. Robinson is likely to be a potential source of stress and trauma for Bobby. Unless this conflict can be shielded from the boy, he'll surely develop severe psychological conflicts and ambivalent feelings regarding his affection for both parents. Should this occur, he will require professional psychotherapeutic intervention from time to time. The potential for continued conflict appears to be great. It is thus also my belief that all parties should be referred for appropriate conciliation."

With that, John rested and turned the questioning over to Frank Gomez. The man had a mountain to climb, but he was anxious to get going.

"Dr. Elinson," he began, "about how many hours did you spend talking with Mr. Robinson?"

Elinson told him that he had spent about two hours with

each of the parents.

"Amazing," Frank said, "And in so short a time you were able to come to know the parties so well. It even appears that you know Mr. Robinson better than his wife does although she lived with him for three years!"

Elinson responded that his tests had a high degree of reliability, but on further cross-examination he was forced to admit that they weren't foolproof.

Gomez continued, "You stated that Mr. Robinson has a degree in psychology. Would he then have taken a course in psychological testing?"

"I suppose so," responded the doctor.

"What kind of advantage would such knowledge give him over Mrs. Robinson, who has not had a single psychology course and who is unfamiliar with such tests?" Frank asked.

"A test like the MMPI has a lie scale built in. Mrs. Robinson was caught lying several times. Mr. Robinson would have been more careful, on the lookout for such test items." Elinson said.

Again Frank asked, "Do you have any reason to believe that Mr. Robinson lied, too?"

"Not really," the doctor responded.

Gomez pressed on. "You said that Mr. Robinson described himself as being a traditional and Conservative Jew."

"That's right," Elinson said.

"Did you know that Mr. Robinson has, for the past two years of his marriage, fasted during the Moslem month of Ramadan, for 30 days each year from sunrise to sunset on each of those days?" Frank asked.

"I wasn't aware of that," Elinson admitted.

"Is that what you'd call traditional Conservative Judaism?" Frank sneered.

"No, I wouldn't. However, I have read Mr. Robinson's book; and I believe that if he so fasted, it would probably have been done to gain credibility with the Moslems that he was attempting to reconcile with his own people. From what Mr. Robinson has also told me, it should be noted that he has had second thoughts about his book. I am sure that this man is now in the process of a return to more traditional Jewish beliefs," the doctor said with confidence.

Frank asked the doctor for his opinion of *The Great Christ Debate*. He wanted to know if Dr. Elinson didn't find the book a bit strange.

"No, I didn't find the book strange at all," Elinson said. Then he added, "It was a bit hard to read at times, but Mr. Robinson did a very scholarly job. Personally, I admire the man quite a lot for what he's trying to accomplish. I only hope that he doesn't give it all up."

"Is there any reason," Frank wanted to know, "for you to believe that he will give it up? After all, the book cost this man his home and his wife, not to mention possession of his son up until this time."

After a sigh, Elinson responded. "Mr. Robinson feels as if the more he came to accept Jesus, the more his wife and Christian in-laws came to reject him. I'm afraid that to a certain extent, when Carmen left him he projected onto Jesus the blame for the failure of the marriage. According to my notes, he quoted a verse . . . Luke 14:26, that had Jesus say that you couldn't be his disciple unless you hated your family members."

Frank decided to take another tact. "Did you know," he asserted, "that when Mr. Robinson ran off to Israel he left no provision for the financial care of his son . . . that he made no provision for payment of the mortgage, or of the car . . . that he left all debts to Mrs. Robinson while he frolicked all over the Middle East and Europe? Do you think that such behavior is what should be expected of a mature and responsible individual?"

Elinson stated that it was easy to pass judgment when you're not in the other guy's shoes. He also pointed out that the trip was necessary in that it gave Steve a chance to sound out his ideas as presented in the book. Anyway, he said, Steve had only been gone for six weeks.

Steve turned to his lawyer and whispered, "We've got to set the record straight about not having sent support. I *did* send it and Carmen knows it! And as for the house, she could have rented it out. She didn't even try. She was the one who wanted the whole thing. She was the one who had the car, too. The truth was that she didn't even try to solve any financial problems."

"Keep your cool," John urged. "It's not our turn now. We'll try to bring all that out later if we can."

Frank continued his harangue. It was, he knew, best to attack an opponent when the person was not free to answer for himself.

"So what we have here, Your Honor, is a man who deserts his family, runs off to Israel leaving them with all the bills, and all for a book that he now doesn't even believe in anymore! Moving on, you stated, Doctor Elinson, that there were a number of responses by the child about being hit by his mother. Yet, when the boy was in the waiting room, you said not that his mother was kissing him, but that he was kissing her."

"That's right," Elinson replied.

"Did you ever see any marks on the boy?" Frank asked.

Elinson told him that none were visible. Gomez went on:

"And you stated, that Bobby knew you by your name."

"Yes," the doctor answered.

"When Mrs. Anderson came to Carmen's mother's house, according to the H.R.S. report, Bobby ran up to her with a statement about wanting to live with his father. Isn't it possible that Mr. Robinson, a trained psychologist, succeeded in conditioning his son to turn against his mother in front of Mrs. Anderson and in front of you? And isn't it possible that Bobby's real feelings were expressed not in your testing room, but out in your waiting room instead?"

There was an expression of self-content as Gomez finished the above query. Elinson's answer, however, was immediate.

"No," the doctor said. "It might be possible for Mr. Robinson to fool me. He does have an intimate knowledge of psychological testing. But it would not be possible for a three-year-old to hide his true feelings on a battery of tests. This child wants very much to live with his father."

Frank next wanted to know if Dr. Elinson had been able to determine anything about the child's views on religion.

Dr. Elinson told the Court that the boy did, on a very primitive level, identify with the Jewish faith. This was quite surprising, he stated, because the lad was inundated with Christian propaganda throughout the day, most days due to Theresa's constant viewing of the Christian Broadcast Network. In fact, his grandmother seldom talked about anything but Jesus.

When Gomez heard that Bobby was not thrilled with Christianity, he tried to blame the child's lack of enthusiasm on his father's conditioning. He suggested that Steve had told the boy that Mommy and Daddy weren't together any more due to Jesus.

By the time Dr. Elinson was finished testifying, his expert-witness fees had grown to $1,700. It had been necessary to have him in court that day not merely to further enhance Steve's case, but because the reports he had written for the Court were not admissible unless he himself had come in to answer questions about them. The same was true of Martha Anderson's report, but there wasn't time enough to call her that morning. In fact, by the time Dr. Elinson had finished testifying, there was time left for only one more witness for Steve's side, Dr. Garnet. Steve could have put Anderson on the stand but had kept his boss waiting outside now for three hours so he called him in instead.

The principal was "a good old country boy" who was proud of the large collection of trophies that Coach Robinson's teams had graced the school display case with. He testified that Steve was an excellent, well-loved teacher and coach, detailed all the man's accomplishments, and was finished giving his presentation in five minutes.

Judge Watts agreed to let Gomez call a witness before lunch, so Theresa was next on the stand. The woman described how the marriage had gone bad after Steve had become obsessed with his book, how he broke into her house to kidnap Bobby after Carmen had pulled out, and how he had embarrassed her frequently with his foul mouth on her lawn or by fighting her elder sons when he came to pick up Bobby and found that Carmen was "five minutes late with the baby." She summed up her opinion of Steve by stating that she thought he was a dangerous man.

John then began his cross-examination.

"Isn't it a fact," he asserted, "that Carmen fails to have Bobby ready for his father's visitation once or twice every month?"

"I haven't been counting," Theresa replied.

"And isn't it a fact that Carmen is often not five minutes late, but four or five hours late instead?" he asked.

"I don't actually put a stopwatch on my daughter," she retorted. Then she added, "Sometimes there may have been problems like that, but not often. Her car breaks down a lot."

John then asked whether or not Carmen had been very late on the days that Steve had done battle with the brothers. Theresa alleged that her daughter's car had suffered a flat tire on each of those days.

"On the day of the last fist fight did anyone at your house call Steve a Kike?" John asked.

"I don't remember," Theresa answered.

"Isn't it a fact," John continued, "that it was not until Mr. Robinson was called a Kike that the fight started?"

"There was a lot of name calling that day. I don't remember who called who what," she said.

"You have two children still in school don't you?" John inquired.

"Yes. And they both get good grades," she added.

"Do they?" John asked sarcastically. " And what do you call good grades?"

"They both get B's and C's," Theresa answered smugly.

"I impeach this witness, Your Honor!" John exclaimed. He then asked that he be given permission to call in Dr. Garnet, who was still in the waiting room talking to Steve's mother. John had subpoenaed the grades of both of Theresa's young children, and Dr. Garnet was carrying them with him.

Over the protests of Gomez who argued that Garnet was finished testifying, Watts allowed the grades of both to be read to the Court. What they showed was that the two were "D" average students with no grades higher than "C" in any area. With that, Theresa was dismissed and the Court adjourned for lunch.

In the afternoon Carmen's brothers testified, as did a number of her friends including the girl who had fixed her up with Steve for their first date. It soon became apparent that there were many who would not get to testify, including Martha Anderson. Gomez told the judge that he wanted to exercise his right to challenge her report, and he stated that Carmen's step-father, Raul, a DC-10 pilot for Sabena Airlines of Belgium, was out of the country. Raul had something critical to say in testimony. Gomez wanted a continuance.

Steve began to feel a sinking feeling in the pit of his gut as he realized that the strain would not end that day. Judge Watts called for his calendar and scheduled another full day of testimony for January 20th, 1981, four months away.

"Your Honor," said John, "this man has endured terrible visitation rights and all expert testimony given today has indicated that he is the primary psychological parent. The visitation guidelines that he has been forced to live by are hard not only on him, but on the child as well. We beg the

Honorable Court to improve those rights during the interim period before the next court date."

"Done," said the judge. "From now until the January hearing, the father will have visitation rights every Wednesday afternoon at 3:30 P.M. until the following Thursday morning at 8:00 A.M. and on alternating weekends from Friday afternoon at 3:30 P.M. until the following Monday morning at 8:00 A.M."

Steve's face lit up like a Roman candle. This was a vast improvement over the eight hours per week that he had previously been allowed.

Gomez in turn moved that the marriage be dissolved then rather than in January. Watts agreed and the five magic words were uttered by Carmen. Court was then adjourned.

Steve reckoned that he would see Bobby some time during the day for eight out of nine days and then not again for five days. This was an arrangement he could live with.

Steve's mother was happy for her son, but still chose to ruin his day with a promise that she wouldn't return to spend another day sitting bored out of her wits in the waiting area. No amount of arguing could sway her, and Steve could only hope that Elinson's testimony would outweigh her absence.

— 5 —
THE INITIAL VERDICT

The months between hearings were pleasant but busy ones for Steve. It had appeared that Judge Watts had been favorably impressed, and there was every reason to hope that the final outcome would be a good one. Gomez, however, had listed a troublesome letter in his pretrial catalog that would involve some research to answer. Steve had written the letter to the Shah of Iran just after *The Great Christ Debate* had been published. The correspondence was to be given to the Shah, along with a copy of the new book, in an effort to get the Shah to allocate some funds for advertising Steve's work. The letter called Christianity a blasphemous religion, and it stated that Steve would do what he could to help ensure its downfall in America and its replacement by Islam. This wasn't likely to endear Robinson to the judge.

What the writer needed was documentation linking Carmen's stepfather (Raul) to Cuban Brigade 2506, for the key to answering the charges to be made concerning the letter were intertwined with Raul's efforts to overthrow Castro.

It was true that Steve had written the letter which Raul

had photocopied. But it was also true that the letter was phrased the way that it had been because Raul had asked Steve to help paint him as a Muslim sympathizer.

Raul was in charge of procuring illegal arms for the anti-Castro Brigade. Oh yes, they had once been the darling of the C.I.A., but not anymore. Now they had to get arms from whatever anti-communist source they could, and who was more anti-communist than the Shah? So Raul had asked Steve for a copy of his book and a letter of introduction that he would give to the Shah's agents in London. The request had been granted by the author in October of 1978, two months before Carmen's departure. Steve had written anti-Castro propaganda for Raul and his Brigade before, so he hadn't suspected that a second purpose of the request was to make a chump out of him in court when the time came, now over two years later. Raul had stabbed him in the back. He was also now financing Carmen's legal costs. For this, Steve felt, there had to be revenge, and he had done much to make the man's life as uncomfortable as possible during the preceding months.

When court was in session on January 20th, the judge started out by asking what the case was about. Steve knew right away that he was in trouble for the old man seemed to have completely forgotten every bit of testimony that he had heard four months before. Elinson's beautiful backing was now lost in the shuffle of papers on the "bulldog's" desk.

John tried as best he could to restore the judge's memory and then called in Mrs. Anderson. By now it had been eight months since she had seen Steve, and her memory was also somewhat diminished by the span of time, a fact that kept her support for him from being as solid as it might have been or even had been in her report.

Martha stated the major concerns of the parties as best she could recollect. The mother saw the father as a dreamer who had visions that he was the Messiah or a prophet of some kind. Carmen thought that he was trying to instill hate in the boy. None of these things were, however, apparent to her in the interview.

"The father," she said, "was a responsible man who only wanted to get better access to his son. He stated that Mrs. Robinson kept the boy from him only to spite him. Mr. Robinson felt that the mother doesn't truly love her son, which is why she often dumps the boy on her mother rather than allowing him to stay with his father while she's out of town flying. He said that he would be more qualified to raise the child because he was more educated than Bobby's mother and because his wife was too much a jet-set swinger to be an effective mother."

John asked her if she found anything in her interview of Carmen to support Steve's concerns.

"I don't know if Mrs. Robinson is really a swinger. I do feel that she has sincere affection for the child, but I'm concerned about her desire to keep the father from having any contact whatsoever. It seems that Mr. Robinson has to fight . . . physically fight with members of her family . . . to get to see his son. It's for this reason that I feel it would be best to place the child with his father. Bobby loves both parents, but he appears to have far more affection for his dad. I see so many men completely abandon their children when a marriage ends, probably due in part to the rough time that fathers have when they get to court. It's refreshing to find a father who cares so much about his son. That's why I don't hesitate to recommend full custody for Mr. Robinson."

John then turned Martha over to Gomez for questioning.

"Mrs. Anderson," he started in, "you said that the basis of your opposition to giving custody to Mrs. Robinson was that she was anxious to deny visitation privileges to the father."

"That's correct," Martha replied.

"Mrs. Robinson has now, eight months after you visited with her, adjusted to the fact that Mr. Robinson will have liberal visitation. She no longer desires to keep Robert from his father; in fact she realizes that such visitation is in the best interest of her son. Does this affect your decision?"

"Well, I guess so. Eight months is a long time. I'm glad to hear that she feels this way," Martha said.

Steve turned to John and whispered, "My, isn't it big of my ex to promise the visitation that the judge has already ordered now that the case is going against her? I can't believe that Anderson is being fooled so easily by that crocodile smile of Gomez!"

John reassured his client that he thought the judge wouldn't be taken in so easily.

"So," Gomez continued, "knowing what you do now, you're no longer ready to recommend a switch of custody at this time?"

"I'm not as sure as I was last May," she said.

"Thank you, Mrs. Anderson. I have no further questions for this witness, Your Honor. I'd like to call in Raul Gonzales at this time," Gomez said with a heave of relief.

Raul was a G. Gordon Liddy type of man, a mercenary

pilot who'd been only partially tamed by the airline industry. It seems likely that "Rambo" of later fame could have taken a lesson or two from the man, and Steve felt badly about having to face him as an adversary. Both were ardent anti-communists, and it was a tragedy that these two one-time friends now spent so much time plotting against each other.

Steve had managed to dig up speeches that he had written for Raul, some of which had been published in America, others which had been broadcast from Samoza's Nicaragua into Cuba with the hope of instigating an insurrection there.

Raul was sworn in and began to attack Steve as an anti-Christ when Gomez produced the letter that Steve had spent so much time preparing to defend against.

"I have here," the Latin attorney said, "a copy of a letter addressed to the Shah of Iran. Do you recognize it?"

Before Raul could even open his mouth, John objected.

"Your Honor, " John said, "this is a xerox copy of a letter. Under the Evidence Code, it states very clearly that photocopies are not admissible evidence. They are much too easy to alter. We must insist that unless Mr. Gomez can produce the actual letter, he be barred from discussing the letter or attempting to use it in any way as evidence."

"Objection sustained," Watts bellowed.

Steve turned to his attorney and congratulated him on a job well done. "You earned your salary with that one," he said.

Gomez was not, however, to be easily deterred. One way or another, he managed to drag out the general sense of the letter from Raul, thus forcing John to counter by presenting all the military aspects of Raul's trip to the Shah's representatives in London. After an hour it looked as if Raul's testimony had been neutralized, but the truth was that Watts had read the letter anyway for it was in Gomez's pretrial catalog that the judge had studied before entering court that day. The old man didn't like what he'd read, and he didn't give a hoot about any excuses.

When all the witnesses had been called for both sides, except for the two parents themselves, Carmen was asked why she wanted custody.

"Well, Your Honor," she said, "I feel that I should have custody because at one time Bobby was part of my body. We were one. I was the one who had to carry him to term those nine months and I was the one that had to suffer the pain of a Caesarean section to deliver him. I got the scar, not his father. He only knew how to run off to Israel while we were separated, leaving me with his child and no support. If you give him my baby, he'll run off to Israel, and I'll never see my boy again. You must keep him from stealing my baby. The man lives in a fantasy world and he can't be trusted. He's irresponsible and a quitter. I don't want my son raised to be a quitter."

"What do you mean by that?" Frank asked.

"He joined the Navy, and then he quit it. He went to podiatry school, and he quit that, too. He quit the Reserves. His book has sold few copies, and he doesn't believe in it anymore. Not even his own parents support him. He couldn't even get them to come here today to testify on his behalf. The man's a loser."

"What kind of a husband was Mr. Robinson?" Gomez prompted.

"I don't care what any psychologist or social worker says. I lived with him. I know him better than anyone else possibly could. He did think he was a prophet which is why his parents refused to come to support him. They knew how crazy he was and still is.

"Steve was terrible with money, too. We were always broke. He bought me nothing. I had to get a job when he sold the house to pay for the publication of his book. All he ever cared about was his ridiculous book."

"Your witness, Mr. Oskowitz."

"Mrs. Robinson, on the average, how many nights per week are you away from home?" John asked.

"I don't know. Sometimes I'm not away at all. For nearly half the month I don't have to fly. My work comes in concentrated spurts. When I'm home I have plenty of time to spend with the baby," Carmen said.

John pressed her again on the question but got nowhere, so he introduced a subpoenaed copy of her work schedule for the previous six months. He asked her if she recognized it as hers, but she said she couldn't remember whether all the flights listed on it were really ones that she had worked.

"According to this schedule," John stated, "in the past two weeks you have overnighted once in Seoul, once in San Francisco, once in Seattle, once in Minneapolis, and three times in Chicago. Can you just confirm that much?"

"No, one airport looks pretty much like another. I was never really very good in geography and I haven't paid attention. A flight is just a flight to me. It's no big deal," she said as if bored by all the queries.

Annoyed, John turned and told the judge that the schedule had been certified by Northwest Orient as being hers. Watts somewhat reluctantly agreed to have the evidence admitted.

Oskowitz decided to turn the Court's attention back to the book next. He asked if Carmen had read it, and she admitted that she hadn't because the topic didn't interest her even if it was dedicated to her.

"Did you oppose selling the first marital home to finance publication?" he asked.

The woman said that she did, but that she went along with it because she knew the book was "an important expression" for her husband.

"You agreed to help him publish the book. Then why did you leave him when his dream had been realized?" the attorney asked.

"Because I got tired of hearing him fight with my mother about it all the time. I didn't have to read it. He never let me forget about what was in it, not even for a moment."

"Your attorney said that Mr. Robinson wanted all Christians in America to convert to Islam. Did your husband ever try to convert you to that faith?" John asked.

"No, he wanted me to become a Jew. He saw Islam as an adequate faith for the Gentiles but Judaism as the faith right for us. He wanted me to be a Jew because he said that a house divided against itself cannot stand," Carmen answered.

"Did you become a Jew?" the lawyer asked.

"No, I'm Christian . . . a Catholic," Carmen replied.

John had finished questioning Carmen, and now there was but one person left to be heard before the verdict was rendered, Steve himself. John asked him the same question that Carmen had been given, why he wanted custody.

Although the father normally prided himself in logic, his response was surprisingly emotional. He also made the mistake of focusing on negatives.

"That woman over there wants custody for one reason only, to lord it over me. She doesn't love her son one bit. In fact, the woman doesn't even know how to love. But she does think she's obligated to fight for our child in order to keep others from saying that she's abandoned him.

"Look at the attendance record that Carmen has had over the past year of legal squabbling. Twice she failed to show at the mediator's, twice again at the psychologist's and once again at a general master's hearing. Until only this day, she has refused to budge from her anti-visitation stand though everyone kept telling her that such a position would cost her custody. Even now I've heard a change in position from her attorney, but not from her own lips.

"I want custody because Bobby and I have a love for each other that Carmen can never match. She failed to give him a sufficient amount of physical nurturing when bonding naturally occurs during the first year. At that time Bobby was always on my chest or lap. I gave him his morning bottle; I came home to feed him lunch; and I put him to sleep on my chest every night. That's why, despite the limited visitation my son and I have endured these past two years, I remain the primary psychological parent in Bobby's eyes, and in the eyes of all the expert witnesses who have studied us. Bobby will never be truly happy until he lives under my roof, nor will I ever cease my efforts to make it so until it is so." With that Steve sat back and waited for the next question.

"Do you think you're a prophet?" John asked.

"Certainly not. I never claimed such a thing, but I do hope that somehow God will guide me to help all religions get along better. Carmen has said she thinks I believe I'm the Messiah. No man, not even Jesus, and certainly not I, can in accordance with the Jewish religion claim to be the Messiah until he accomplishes the most important task of the Anointed One, namely delivery of the end of war to this planet and the ushering in of an everlasting age of peace. No, I'm not the Messiah, but I, and my son, and every Jew, and every thinking human being must strive to become the Messiah for what does it matter if billions of us fail so long as one of us succeeds?"

There were a few more questions for Steve to answer. He spoke of child support he had sent from Israel, of his need to finish the book so Carmen would stop calling him a "quitter," how he planned to take care of Bobby while he was at work, and the visitation he was willing to grant Carmen should he win.

When it was Frank's turn to grill him, Steve had to answer a number of questions about how he viewed women. Gomez tried to pain the author as a "male chauvinist" because Steve had shown in his book that a similar attitude towards women had existed in the Old Testament, New Testament and Koran. Watts intervened and told Gomez that Mr. Robinson couldn't be held responsible for what the Scriptures contained.

Gomez took a last shot before the judge ruled.

"Your Honor, this man has done a good job of fooling the psychologist and the social worker. He has not, however, fooled his wife, nor has he fooled his parents whose absence speaks elegantly for his fanaticism. I hope that you too will not be deceived."

Gomez sat down and Watts began to speak.

"I'm ready to rule. I find that both parents are fit to have custody of the child, Robert Altair Robinson, and I am going to order joint custody, primary residential status shall be with . . . the mother."

Steve felt like a meat ax had just split his head in two. The judge continued: "The father to have liberal visitation, namely every Wednesday afternoon at 3:30 until Thursday morning at 8:00 A.M. and every other weekend from Friday afternoon at 3:30 until Sunday evening at 6:00 P.M."

That Steve immediately recognized to be a *reduction* in visitation rights from his previous weekend rights which had extended until Monday morning.

"Both parents," the judge added, "shall have equal rights concerning the care, health, and welfare of the minor child. The father shall also have alternating holiday overnight visitation rights, and he shall pay the mother child support in the amount of forty dollars per week. This Court shall retain jurisdiction over this case should any future problems arise."

Steve tried to challenge the return time on weekend visitation, pointing out that the mother lived one block from his Monday morning work place, but 25 miles from his home in Homestead.

"Visitation will be as I ordered," bellowed the judge. "As for you, young lady, any future trouble and I reserve the right to switch full custody over to this man." The judge then rose and started out of the Court.

Steve clenched his fist and yelled at Watts, "I'm gonna appeal this damn decision. You make me pay thousands for a court-appointed psychologist, and then you don't heed his advice or the social worker's! I can't live with these visitation guidelines!"

"Good day," Watts replied, and he was gone.

Carmen and Gomez left the courtroom next while Steve just sat there in a state of shock, trying to understand all the implications of the new order. He was more furious about the visitation reduction than anything else, and he knew that Bobby would not be happy either about the early return to his mother's place on Sundays.

"It's like I said," John rationalized in a subdued voice, "the child's of tender years, you're a man and a Jew to boot. Give it a couple of years. When the boy is six or seven, you can try again."

Outside the courthouse the losers began to walk back towards the attorney's office. Oskowitz looked like he had just been through a war. He had forgotten to shave that morning, and he had ripped his jacket under the armpit as he had gotten out of his car just before the hearing had started. He looked terrible, and his client was now wondering whether or not such an appearance hadn't worked against him in court that day.

About a block from the courthouse, a nun stopped Robinson to ask for a donation for Christ. He ignored her, but he felt like strangling the woman. He felt like telling off his attorney, too, but did not. The two men would never see or speak to each other again.

When Robinson next picked up Bobby at his mother's, Carmen was waiting outside to speak with him. Bobby rushed into his father's arms and asked, "Did we win, Daddy? Can I live with you now?"

He picked his son up and told him, "No, we won some things, but you'll still have to go back and forth and live most of the time with Mommy." Then he turned to his ex-wife and said, "It's not fair. All the expert witnesses on my side and you get him only because you have female genitalia. Bobby won't be of tender years forever. I won't accept the Sunday return on visitation. I'm going to appeal the case for sure unless we can reach an agreement to restore the Monday drop-off. Look, if you give me what I want, I'll pay for Bobby's health insurance. The judge forgot to include it in the order. What do ya say?"

Carmen was too drained to fight on. She agreed to his terms.

In the car on the way back to Steve's home, Bobby put his head on his father's lap and his dad gently stroked it. The man tried to reassure his son that everything would be all right. "I guess we didn't make out so bad after all. I've got joint custody now. You'll still see me a lot, and Mommy and I have quit fighting."

At home that night Robinson decided to alter the usual sequence of bedtime events. Before he had always tickled and hugged his little boy, but now he would begin to indoctrinate him.

"What religion are you, Bobby?"

"I'm Jewish like you, Daddy."

"Then," Steve asserted, "you must start to learn Hebrew for the power to be a good Jew lies in the knowledge of our language."

The boy was curious about why that was, so the father told him about how it was that the Torah had been revealed in Hebrew to Moses on the Mountain of God. He also informed his son that to be Jewish the boy would have to be willing to convert because Carmen wasn't a Jew. Yes, Bobby had received a Brith Milah, but the will to be a Jew had to be inscribed in his brain and on his heart even as it had been upon the token of his manhood.

"Repeat after me," Steve urged. "Shema Yisrael Adonoy Elohaynoo Adonoy Echod . . . Hear, Oh Israel, the Lord our God, the Lord is One . . . This teaches us that there is only One God. You will in your lifetime hear lots of people say different things about God. Some will say there is no God. These people think they were created by an accident. Others will say that God has three forms, or that there are many gods. But if you really wish to be a Jew like your father, you must never lose sight of the belief that there is *One* God, an indivisible super Spirit who made us and who always watches over us."

"What's a Spirit, Daddy?"

"It's hard to describe. I guess it's like a person without a body. But God isn't a person. In fact, we aren't even allowed to try to picture what He is. That's one of His commandments. He told us not to make an image of anything in heaven."

The boy eagerly repeated his father's magical words. On each visit Steve read another Bible story to his son before turning out the lights. The last words uttered by the lad each night and the first words he recited each morning were always the Shema.

— 6 —
INTERIM YEARS OF PEACE

"*Shalom*" means hello, good-by and peace. The next three years were blessed with peace. During the first summer to follow the trial, Carmen allowed Steve to take their son to a camp named Shalom in central Florida where he worked as a head counselor.

Bobby was now four years old, and he was allowed to sleep with a cabin full of slightly older kids while his father was in the next room. The little guy proved to be a real champ at water skiing.

The camp was nearly all Jewish, but Bobby's mother didn't seem to mind. She even flew him up to be with his father, who at the time appeared to be more interested in fishing, hiking, canoeing and other campy things than in theological matters. Of course, every few weeks when a new batch of kids would show up, he'd be tempted around the campfires at night to spin yarns of the reincarnation of Sabbatai Sevi. There were many questions about the scar on his neck. It was more fun to spook the kids about being "the gilgol of the Mystical Messiah" than to tell them about a lousy old cyst. Whenever he got to the part about the sword being placed over Sevi's neck, he loved to send chills down their little spines by running his hand along his own long, wide and hideous scar.

Everybody loved him because he was such a scary storyteller. He had a tale about everything. One night he terrified the campers by letting them know about how it was that Big Foot had killed and eaten three kids the summer before. When he finished all the gruesome details, he slipped away to the wood shop where he carved two giant wooden feet. That same night he canoed across the lake and, with the false feet strapped to his own, went about making giant foot prints all over the sand on the far shore. When the campers rowed over the next morning, you could hear screams of terror for miles around as they ran for their boats after finding the "proof" that Big Foot did indeed exist and stalk the area. Bobby participated in the whole plot and he loved it (though Steve did eventually tell the kids what he did).

The man's relationship with Carmen was rapidly improving, and he tried once again to get her to come back. At one point she agreed to date him with his son at Disney World; but when the big day arrived, she backed out after having undergone a major battle with her mother about it. For months it seemed as if their first date was just around the corner, but somehow he never quite managed to pull it off.

Robinson's hopes for a sailboat were vanquished by all the legal bills he had paid, but (with Bob Finnerty's assistance) he was able to afford a new lakefront townhouse in Homestead.

Many Jews will attend services when they move into a new community. They hope to meet fellow Jews, or if single, to meet Jews of the opposite sex. Steve was no exception. Contrary to what he had heard, there were Jews in the South Florida town, but most of them were thirty years his senior.

While there were no young beauties at the Homestead Jewish Center, he quickly grew to appreciate the old men of the Saturday morning service. For all the theology that he had written of, and for all the religious history that he had mastered, his skills in Hebrew prayer were weak. Here they would rapidly grow.

The old-timers were parent figures to him. They filled a void that had opened ever since the day that his parents had failed to show up in court. He felt as though he could never forgive them, and yet they were with him in his dreams night after night.

Two congregants grew to be his favorites, Morris Levy and Harold Markowitz. Each did whatever he could to nourish Steve's complete return to the traditional Jewish fold, but the spiritual soul of the congregation was Michael Klein, the handsome, thirty-year-old acting rabbi.

Mike had been blessed with a yeshiva education, but he still thought highly of Robinson's book. In fact, Mike was the only one there that Steve even told about the book for the next three years. With time the two men became the best of friends.

On alternating Friday nights, Bobby accompanied his father to the synagogue. Often the boy would fall asleep in his father's arms right after the wine from the Kiddush prayer would knock him out. But after a few weeks there, the little guy asked Mike for permission to lead the congregation in the Shema. Although still only four years old, he was already becoming a regular "kosher ham." Most people were sure that his father had put him up to the request, but truth was that Bobby thought of the idea all by himself. When he sang for the congregation, the old folks instantly fell in love with their new young cantor, and Bobby soon found that he had a "permanent job." A month later the boy had memorized a longer Hebrew prayer called the "Viyahavta," and a few weeks after that he had added the Kiddush blessing over the wine to his repertoire. After each "performance" he'd be sure to personally shake every congregant's hand. You might have thought the little politician was trying to run for president of the synagogue.

Carmen continued to mellow, extending Steve's visitation rights from the biweekly schedule originally agreed upon to two out of three weekends and then to nearly every weekend. What she could only suspect but was apparently unconcerned about was that Bobby was now in synagogue for an average of 12 days per month including Friday night and Saturday morning services plus Sunday school. Although she would later claim that her flight schedule kept her too busy to take her son to church, the fact was that she still had no interest in religion. Thus the boy was constantly exposed to one side of the religious picture. True, Theresa always had on the "700 Club" or the "Praise the Lord Hour" when her grandson was staying over, but Bobby just plain tuned the stuff out that he was hearing there.

It was a great arrangement for Steve. The time he spent with his son was "quality time." Bobby was receiving a tremendous Jewish education for a child of such tender years. There was only one problem. The boy was always over at his house on weekends, so the father never dated.

Bobby wasn't unaware that his mother might be less than happy about all that he was learning. He would answer her questions about attending synagogue or going to Sunday school, but he'd always be careful not to raise the subject of religion himself while over at his mother's. When served bacon by his mom, he'd hide it in his socks or throw it down the toilet when his mother wasn't looking rather than start a fight over the kosher dietary laws. He was, in effect, becoming a new "Morrano" or secret Jew in his own mother's home.

A year flew by and Steve still hadn't seen a Jewish female under the age of sixty-five in Homestead. Occasionally he'd meet someone Jewish in Kendall, the area that he worked in during the day, but none shared his interest in religion or seemed worth a trip back in the evenings. At last he decided that if he couldn't find a proper Jewish wife, he'd "make one."

The most common place people meet before getting married is in an academic setting. Knowing this, he managed to land a teaching position at the South Dade Adult Education Center in Homestead. The instructor preferred a job teaching science, but none was available so he had to settle for an "ESOL" class where immigrants were taught English as a second language.

On his first night there, he was impressed by the beauty of a number of Korean girls. Another teacher told him that they were all married to servicemen at the Air Force base nearby. "The girls marry G.I.'s overseas and then divorce them soon after they get to the States. All they want is American citizenship," the other teacher (an elderly woman) said and then added, "but what they get is American poverty. Most of their cases are tragic."

There was one girl that particularly caught his eye that first night. She didn't look a day over fifteen, but she was an exquisite beauty who wore an orchid in her long, flowing jet-black hair. Ok Chu Kim had been her Korean name, but now she called herself by the name "Ruth."

The girl didn't speak much English, and at first Steve thought that she was too young for a thirty-four-year-old man to approach. Even if she were eighteen, he reasoned, she'd have to be some serviceman's wife.

After class each night for the next two weeks, he could think of nothing but the girl with the orchid. When he finally did speak to her, he learned that she was single, adopted by her sister's G.I. husband, and twenty years old. Still, he couldn't bring himself to ask her for a date.

It was true that he had been determined to convert someone, but a girl who could barely speak English would be almost impossible to bring over. To be a Jew wasn't a matter of having someone pour water on your head. There was a vast body of knowledge for a convert to digest and a multitude of laws to accept before appearing in front of a Bet Din or rabbinical tribunal. And yet, as each night passed, he knew that he was falling more and more in love with her. Ruth wasn't actually in Steve's class, but she was in the adjoining room. One night her teacher was out, and he found himself covering that class as well as his own. There was Ruth before him, still with a flower in her hair. He started teaching with nothing but the girl on his mind, then turned and asked her how to say "I love you" in Korean.

"Nanune tongshina sarong hamnida," Ruth said in a

quiet voice. He gazed at her with longing eyes and then said loudly, "Nanune tongshina sarong hamnida," and all the other Korean women in class began to roar with laughter as Ruth just lowered her eyes with embarrassment.

"My God," he thought, "if I marry this girl, I'll be jumping out of the frying pan and into the fire." Everyone at school knew that he was nuts about her, save Ruth herself who thought he was joking in class. She saw him only as a funny-looking, bald old man with a slight pot belly and a good sense of humor.

After two months of trying his best to avoid her during the break between classes, he finally found himself seated at her table making small talk. She was telling him about her career plans, but he was fixated on her lips which were the most provocative that he'd seen anywhere. He could resist no longer and asked her for a phone number.

Ruth was somewhat surprised by the teacher's actions but not offended by them.

"I give phone number," she said, "but you must ask big sister permission date me. Suki say O.K., is O.K. Must give older sister respect."

When he called later that night, sure enough Suki got on the phone. "How olda you?" she asked. Steve told her, and then was hit by her next question. "How muchee money you make?" The amount was high enough, so Suki gave her blessing to the first date with the "old man."

Steve finally sprang for a babysitter that Saturday night and picked up Ruth at 8:00 P.M. She was living in a rundown part of Homestead. There were junked cars and barking dogs all over the area, but Ruth was dressed to kill in a beautiful blue gown. True to form, an orchid adorned her hair. The Shalimar perfume she was wearing made him want to skip the preliminaries and settle in on love making the instant he caught a whiff. They went out for a dinner at the Holiday Inn where Steve did all the talking while Ruth pretended to understand.

After dinner Steve took her back to his home to meet Bobby. The boy was still awake, waiting for his customary bedtime story. When he first laid eyes on his father's date, he fell for her just as his dad had.

"Wow," he said, "Daddy told me you were pretty. He sure knows how to pick 'em!"

At first Ruth just watched as the boy snuggled up to his dad in bed. Steve decided to read the Biblical story of "Ruth." Then, enchanted by the tale of her namesake, she climbed in and put her head on the father's other shoulder while he finished the book. Bobby soon fell asleep and now the two new lovers were left gazing at each other face to face.

Ruth began to see her date as a loving father, something that she'd missed during the past few years in America. The instructor knew that he couldn't hold onto her by reason of his looks alone, for he was aware that he wasn't an overly attractive man. As a psychology major, he also knew that most women are subconsciously attracted to a "father figure," so he decided to play that angle to the hilt. Ruth was a "little girl" who needed someone to protect her and to teach her all about the strange new land that destiny had led her to. Steve wanted to be the man who could satisfy those needs.

The "old man" didn't push his luck that night. He behaved as a perfect gentleman and soon drove her back to

Suki's apartment. As he went to kiss her good night, he was still afraid that he'd wind up with another problem marriage if he continued to see her, so he warned her, "If you want to date me again, you're gonna have to become Jewish, like the Ruth we read about tonight."

"I ask Suki for permission to become Jewishee," Ruth promised.

"Is she a Christian?" Steve asked.

"No, she Buddha person. In my home in Korea, some Christian persons, some Buddha persons. Some both. Suki probably not mind if we have Jewishee person, too."

The next "date" for the couple featured a trip to meet Rabbi Hoffman at Temple Beth Am, a large Reform congregation. Steve arrived at 6:30 P.M. that Monday, and once again his love was dressed in a beautiful evening gown. The problem, however, wasn't that she was overdressed. The problem was that she was wearing a huge gold cross around her neck and two gold cross earrings!

"You can't wear those to meet the rabbi!" Steve exclaimed.

"Why not? They pretty! They real gold! My old boyfriend buy them for me!" Ruth said emphatically.

"Jewish people don't believe in Jesus," he told her.

This Ruth did not like. Not that she cared at all about Jesus, but it was a shock for her to learn that her gold was "no good."

"Look," Steve told her, "If the only problem is that your jewelry is no good, I'll take you to Luria's on the way to the rabbi and buy you something gold there, something more appropriate."

With that the two drove off to the jewelry store where

the man purchased a necklace with a lovely gold Jewish star and the Ten Commandments engraved on it. Ruth loved it but was less than totally satisfied because he had failed to replace the earrings, too. Still, she was content enough to begin her instruction that night.

The conversion program at Beth Am was twelve weeks long with mandatory classes and service attendance each week. Ruth's English wasn't up to the speed at which the rabbi taught and though she tried hard, she got little out of the classes. Her new fiance (for Steve had wasted no time before proposing) spent hours after each session attempting to explain what the rabbi had said. Still, all she understood was that "Jews believed in One God. Jesus was neither that God nor His Messiah because he had failed to bring peace."

During the spring break, Robinson took Ruth and his son up to Disney World for a quick vacation. When they returned to Homestead, it was time to make a Passover seder.

The teacher did all he could to set a proper seder table. He was anxious to explain the meaning of the meal, but it was obvious that Ruth was rapidly growing bored by the whole ritual. In fact, by the looks she was sending his way across the table, he could tell she was more interested in making love than in learning about his faith. At any other meal he would have been flattered. But this was something sacred and important to him, and he was disturbed by her attitude. The next day he called Rabbi Hoffman and told him that despite Ruth's completion of their program, and despite his desire to see his love's conversion so they'd be free to marry, he couldn't honestly sanction her entry into the Covenant of Abraham until her comprehension of the faith was more in line with what he expected of a proper Jewish wife. The rabbi had himself once been fond of a Japanese girl. He understood the cultural hurdle that Steve had to get his fiancee over, and he was pleased by the man's sincerity. Hoffman wished them both well.

Ruth was mildly upset when she learned that Steve had "flunked her" on her Jewish studies, but he told her that all wasn't lost and that he still loved her. The solution to their problems, he said, was to return to the Homestead Jewish Center where most of the prayers were in Hebrew and where he hoped that she would learn what Judaism was all about by way of a more traditional service. Ruth had a gift for studying languages, and so it was that after a few weeks those around her were startled to find that she had memorized the prayers and was singing in Hebrew better than many of the old women that had been there for years.

The Korean's desire to learn the ancient tongue wasn't all motivated by a pure love for the faith. No indeed, for truth was that she had grown jealous of Bobby who was receiving so many accolades because of all he had mastered in Hebrew.

Although she was twenty, Ruth was like a child in many ways. Steve noticed that she quickly grew upset whenever she felt that he was giving the boy more attention than she was getting. "You didn't tension me!" she would tell him while ready to cry like a little girl. Then, too, there was quite a row until her love decided who got to sit next to him in the car. Bobby had always held the "honored" position before his dad started dating her. Now she sought to replace him, and the boy was concerned that Daddy loved someone more than him. Steve felt like he was always walking a tightrope between the two. He would tell them things like, "I love each of you as I do my two legs. I wouldn't want to get along without either of them and I wouldn't want to be without either of you." A hundred times the answer would be given and a hundred times they would ask the same question the next day. He certainly knew that he was loved. By the way, Ruth got to sit next to him in the car. It wasn't that he loved her more than his son. He didn't know who he loved more. What he did know was that Bobby would never leave him, but there were millions of other guys out there who'd give their right arm to get a knockout like his girl. He couldn't afford to take the chance of losing her, for he feared that any balding, scar-marked, slightly potbellied man like him who could land a girl like her was more than a little bit lucky. She was a prize well worth holding onto, even if it would take another year or two to mold her into the kind of mature woman that he needed for both wife and stepmother to his son.

Eight months after Ruth began to attend services in Homestead, she registered for a Bat Mitzvah class. By now her English and Hebrew were both vastly improved as was her attitude about Judaism. Again she was entered into a conversion program at Temple Samuel where Rabbi Farber immediately appointed Steve as the teacher. After three trips back to see the rabbi, Farber found her to be a walking Jewish encyclopedia, and he made arrangements to have her appear before a Conservative Bet Din. There was by this time so much competition between Ruth and Bobby that the two would often sit in the car and fire Jewish trivia questions back and forth at each other. Both knew far more than the average adult male Jew did, and Steve got more than his share of "nachus" (pleasure) whenever the two would try to impress him by their vast knowledge. At synagogue each week he was congratulated by all for being a great teacher, and it was because of his two beloved students that he was appointed Sunday School Director.

In early March, 1983, Ruth passed her exam before the tribunal with flying colors, received her "mikvah" or ritual immersion, and then was married to her proud instructor on March 25th. The couple had preferred a March 31st wedding date, but Jewish law pertaining to the "counting of the Omer" barred weddings then.

The wedding was a small affair, perhaps forty people being in attendance (including Steve's parents). The newlyweds spent the weekend at a Miami Beach motel but left for the "real honeymoon" in Vail, Colorado, during the spring break, a week later.

For much of the remainder of 1983, all went well for the man and his new family. He joined the Coast Guard Reserves and earned a commission. Ruth, not content at being just a cute "sex object," soon proved that she had a gift for math as well as language. She began college and, in short order, was knee deep in calculus. The future seemed bright, but what the Robinson's were enjoying would soon prove to be only the calm before the storm.

— 7 —
THE BATTLE RESUMES

There was peace until that November. Steve decided to attempt to put together a teen tour to Israel for the following spring. He called his ex to find out if she would allow Bobby to tag along. The response wasn't a friendly one.

Carmen argued that it wasn't safe to travel to Israel and, although it was still before the crazy terrorist outbreaks to follow in later years, no amount of arguing by Steve could sway her from that conviction. He warned her that he was so serious about his desire to show his son the country that he might consider court action to gain permission. That made the woman "see red", and she let him know in no uncertain terms that she was as much opposed to the trip as he was in favor of it. To get the point across, she started to cut into Robinson's unofficial visitation rights. At first she'd leave messages at Steve's school. He'd be all set to pick up his son on a Friday afternoon, only to find out at the last moment that the woman would be keeping Bobby for the weekend. If it was supposed to be her weekend, he didn't mind too much. "It's good," he reasoned, "that she's finally taking more of an interest in our son."

But it wasn't long before the woman began to also keep Bobby on weekends that were supposed to be his. That made him begin to get angry. True, he'd been given visitation for the past few years that was far in excess of what the court order had read, but father and son were by now accustomed to their time together.

In mid-December, 1983, Steve's folks invited him up to their Miami Beach condo to dinner. Ruth put on her prettiest dress, and the two drove over to Theresa's to pick up Bobby. When they got there, Carmen and the boy were waiting out front with Raul, who was washing his car. The ex mercenary took one look at Steve's new wife, who he hadn't seen before, and then congratulated his old friend for finding such "an exquisite beauty." Now though it was true that Carmen was then living with her Catholic boyfriend, Ricardo, it was also true that it bothered her to see Steve so happy with another woman. The Latin had bragged to Steve about how she enjoyed breaking the hearts of her former boyfriends. She knew Steve had been deeply hurt, too, but now believed that he was flaunting his new love. This belief rekindled all the hatred of the last custody fight. When Steve picked up his boy the next time, his son bore ominous news.

"Mom took me to church for Christmas," he told his dad. "Not only that," he continued, "but she forced me to eat pork. She said God gave us pork to eat and it was no sin if I ate it. Besides, she told me that I'm a Catholic because the Jewish religion says the child must take the religion of the mother."

In all the time that he had known Carmen, she had never expressed an interest in the Church. Steve wondered why the sudden change had occurred and postulated that Carmen's new love might have something to do with it. Perhaps the man didn't care to have a little Jew running around his house.

The following weekend was Carmen's. Steve had to wait until the subsequent Wednesday to learn how serious she was about her new faith. It wasn't good. The woman had taken her son to church again for a regular Sunday Mass. She was going back on her pledge to raise Bobby as a Jew, and the father realized that he'd have to go to war again.

Bobby was more than a bit distressed by the turn of events. He hated looking at the Cross because he had begun to view Jesus as the cause of his parent's divorce. Now it seemed to him that the Nazarene was keeping him from seeing his dad as well.

Steve tried to understand Carmen's motives. He knew that his marriage to her had never been recognized by the Church. Perhaps, he thought, she decided to get right with God and the Vatican by attending services. Since she had primary residency what, (Robinson figured she thought) could I do about it if she took Bobby along? After all, she could argue that she certainly had as much right to expose her child to Catholicism as I had to take him to synagogue. She must have thought that even if she were a bit slow to exercise that option, it was still hers. It seemed likely that she viewed the circumcision as a mere medical procedure that I had tricked her into. No longer married to me, I guess she thinks she only has to abide by the court order now and that doesn't include anything about Bobby's religious upbringing.

A few weeks passed. In late January Steve drove over to

Theresa's to pick his son up for that was still the exchange site. Bobby wasn't there and Theresa hadn't heard from Carmen. He drove back to school, checked his message box and found nothing there about his ex keeping the boy that weekend. There was no answer at Ricardo's when he called, and Bobby's school told him that the boy had been in attendance that day but was now nowhere to be found.

For five hours the worried father drove around the neighborhood trying to find his son. Carmen had never kept Bobby before without notifying him. Darkness set in and still there was no sign of the lad. He drove home and tried to call his ex once more. At last she answered the phone.

"I'm keeping Bobby for the weekend," she told him.

"You didn't leave a message," he snapped. "I've been driving around for hours half scared out of my wits that he'd been kidnapped or something. You know what's been going on lately with all the child murders in Miami. Why didn't you tell me before?"

"I don't have to tell you anything," she retorted.

"Look, Carmen," he said, "I won't stand for the garbage you've been dishing out lately. And what's all this Bobby's been telling me about going to church? You promised to raise our son to be a Jew!"

"I promised nothing," she said.

"And," he added, "it's time you started respecting Bobby's feelings about food. I'm talking about pork."

"Bobby eats it all the time. He loves it," she insisted.

"Loves it, hell!" he argued. "The boy throws the stuff out every time you pack ham for lunch. He's been buying fruit and salads for lunch at school for a year now with the allowance I give him. You know damn well that Jews aren't permitted to eat pork, shellfish, or meat mixed with dairy. If Bobby wants to eat only kosher food, why do you have to make it so hard for him?"

"I don't have to answer you. I'm enrolling Bobby in a catechism class. You can't stop me," she told him.

"I'll see you in court, lady. You just bought yourself a brand new custody suit. Enjoy." He hung up the phone on her so hard that he cracked his own receiver.

Steve took a good look at Ruth and wondered whether she'd stick with him through the stressful and expensive legal campaign that he knew lay ahead. Her relationship with Bobby was marginal on a part-time basis. His little "Oogy Boogie" as he called him tended to look at Ruth more like a big sister than a stepmother who should be an authority figure. If Bobby was going to live with her on a full-time basis, that would have to change; and he knew that it's difficult to alter the dynamics of a relationship once they're set.

Ruth was not overjoyed by what had just transpired, but she let him know that, so long as Bobby would start listening to her, it was O.K. to file the suit.

There was one other person to consult before Steve took decisive action, Bobby himself. On Monday morning he drove over to the boy's school and had him pulled from class. The two walked out to a park bench and sat down for a man-to-man talk.

"What happened this weekend?" the father asked.

"What do you think? They made me go to church again and they hit me when I wouldn't kneel there. I said the Shema in Hebrew instead," Bobby told his father.

"That's my boy! Bobby, listen to me and listen good. We have to make a big decision. You're only six and a half, but this is going to be one of the biggest decisions of your life. What do you want me to do about your mother?" Steve wanted to know.

Without hesitating one second, Bobby said, "Fight for custody, Dad. I can't live with her like this. She used to be nice, but ever since she started going to church she's been real mean to me."

"Do you know what another custody fight means?" Steve asked. "Let me tell you," he continued. "It means that I've got to spend thousands of dollars that I don't have . . . and so does your mother, all for lawyers again. There's no guarantee that I'll win. We'll probably be fighting in the court system for a good year, maybe longer. During that time your mother will reduce my visitation to what Judge Watts decreed last time, and she'll fight to reduce it even more than that. You'll be on the front line of this war all the time. Ricardo and your mother can beat you again or deprive you of food whenever you don't want to eat non-kosher meals. We'll have to start all over again with the psychologists and the social workers, too. Every adult you talk to or who asks you a question is a potential witness in court. You must trust no one and be very careful of everything you say until the whole sordid mess is over. For a kid your age, a year can seem like a lifetime. The last battle left me a nervous wreck, and I'll probably get my nervous tic back again.

"It won't be easy for Ruth either. Right now she says she's with us. When the months start to roll by and the legal bills start to mount, I won't be able to buy her any more pretty dresses. She may resent you for it.

"I don't like to have to tell you all these things. But you're my son and I love you too much to lie to you. You have a right to know just what's involved in the decision that we're making here," Steve said.

By now Bobby was in tears. Still, through all the sobbing, he managed to tell his father, "I want you to fight for me. I don't want to live with Mom anymore and I don't like Ricardo. If you love me, you'll do it."

Steve told Bobby that their chances would be better if they'd wait another six years until Bobby was twelve, but the boy wouldn't stand for such a delay. He then told his father that he had started catechism class and asked how to behave there.

"If," Steve said, "you're well-behaved, your catechism teacher will be in court to testify that you enjoyed the class. Do you want that?"

"No way, Dad."

Steve then told him, "To win the case you must become like Daniel, who wouldn't, as a boy, eat the King's food because it was non-kosher, and like Shadrach, Meshach and Abednego, who walked into the fiery furnace and were unharmed because they wouldn't worship a false god but were instead ready to risk all for the real One."

"When I went up to the mountain of God, Mount Sinai," Steve told his son, "I asked God to deliver you into my hand. Perhaps he heard my prayer and just maybe He's about to do what I asked Him to do. But God demands a price for His intervention. When our forefathers were at the Red Sea, it was not until we had enough faith to wade into the waters to the level of our very nostrils that God saw fit to part the sea and let us pass. And before that, it was not until Abraham had raised the knife to sacrifice his son, who did not try to escape from the altar, that God chose to send the ram instead. We must wade into the waters now 'till they reach our very nostrils. You must be prepared to lie upon the altar, and I must be ready to raise the knife. Then, and only then, will God honor our request and free you from your mother's bondage. There are two people coursing through your genes, the Chosen and the Gentiles. The Chosen were picked not because God is biased but because we were prepared to serve Him. Abraham overcame the pagan influence in his past. I hope that you'll find that same spark of our forefather and let it dominate your thoughts and actions."

"I won't let you down if you won't let me down Daddy," Bobby promised. With tears still in his eyes, he returned to class.

— 8 —
TACTICS

Steve called a number of attorneys. By now the going fee varied from one hundred to one hundred fifty dollars per hour. He had just about recovered from the expenses of the last fight and the thought of paying these fees again was horrifying.

"Why can't I file without an attorney?" he wondered. Although somewhat apprehensive about the idea, he knew that most motions and petitions start and end with a certain set format. All one had to do was find the format and then fill in the guts of the thing with what you were trying to say. He decided to go down to the courthouse, pull the old file from his first custody bout, and photocopy every single form filed. Then all he would have to do was pull whatever was needed at the analogous phase of this fight. "Why pay someone else a fortune to do something as simple as that?" he thought.

Carmen wasted no time before hiring one of Miami's most expensive and best-known attorneys. Karl Schmidt, the man she retained, was a heavy-set German immigrant who looked like the kind of fellow you'd expect to find making his living as a professional wrestler. Carmen liked the fact that he was German. Although Schmidt had no strong feelings about Jews, she hoped that Steve would fear him as a heartless Nazi. She was entitled. After all, when Steve hired Oskowitz in 1980, he liked it that the man looked like a shark. You don't want someone representing you that looks like a pussy cat in a fight like this. Carmen made sure to cram Schmidt's calling card into Steve's hand the next time he came over to pick up his son for visitation.

Steve had a gift for her as well when he picked up his son. It was a list of demands coupled with a well-phrased threat. Carmen took the papers and went inside to read. The first page read:

> "We can avoid court if and only if the following conditions are met:
>
> "(1) The old visitation schedule of three weekends per month at my house is resumed. There should be compensatory time on the weekend that you have Bobby.
>
> "(2) You will not dictate where I take him on vacation.
>
> "(3) You will not force him to attend church against his will, and you will respect his right to call himself a Jew.
>
> "(4) You will not force him to eat ham or any other non-kosher food against his will.
>
> "(5) You will not continue to take him on my days without notifying me of your intentions. Said notification should be as it used to be, namely in the form of a request with accompanying discussion of compensa-

tory time.

"(6) If these conditions are not agreeable, I will hire an attorney by the end of the week, or I will file the papers on my own."

The second page was a list of 24 Bible verses coupled with a threat that Steve would teach them to Bobby. Together the group composed those verses which Christianity had always found to be most embarrassing.

Each verse was described in a positive way. It would be necessary for the full verse to be read to the Court before Steve's motives for selecting it would become clear. That was precisely what Steve wanted done, for he was at war now not just with Carmen alone, but "Christ," and with the past nature of his very own soul as well. The list he prepared read as follows:

The Way To Salvation (According To Jesus) .... John 4:21-22

Fulfilled Prophecies By Jesus .... Luke 14:26, Luke 12:51-53, Matthew 10:34-36

Unfulfilled Prophecies By Jesus .... Matthew 16:28, Mark 9:1, Luke 9:27

The Definition Of A False Prophet .... Deuteronomy 18:20-22, Deuteronomy 13:1-4

Adultery As Defined By Jesus .... Mark 10:12

The Consistency Of Paul .... Galatians 5:3 and Acts 16:3

The Love Of Jesus For Gentiles .... Matthew 15:22-26

The Love Of Jesus For His Mother ..... Matthew 12:46-50,
Mark 3:31-35,
Luke 8:20-21

The Strength That Faith In Jesus Gave To Paul .... Romans 7:14-15

The Faith Of "Christ's" Brothers .... John 7:5

An Appraisal Of Jesus By His Followers .... Mark 3:21

Jesus' Claim To Perfection .... Mark 10:17-18,
Luke 18:18-19

The Awesome Punishment Waiting Those Who Speak Against Jesus .... Luke 12:10

The Consistency Of Jesus And Paul On Matters Of Law .... Matthew 5:19 and
Galatians 3:10-13

Protestant Identification Of The Mother Of Harlots .... Revelation 17:3-9
(Wycliffe Bible Commentary, Page 1517)

Ashamed that he had backed so many Christian teachings about Jesus in his old book, Steve now sought to redeem himself in an American court by proving Jesus to be neither God nor Messiah. He would pit his God, known to Christians as the Father, against "their falsely deified Son." Bobby would be placed upon the altar of American justice in an effort to prove that Jesus had no more power than Baal had. In Steve's own mind, he would need to become both modern Abraham and Elijah all wrapped up in one.

Ruth had cautioned her husband against taking such a tact in court. She knew that the judge was a Catholic. The Protestant Commentary Steve referred to in his letter to

Carmen quoted Luther, Calvin, Tyndale and others as identifying the Vatican itself as the Mother of Harlots. She couldn't understand how he could possibly hope to win by insulting Watts and all he believed in. But Steve knew that it would be ever so easy to move for a mistrial and throw Watts off the case if the judge revealed any Catholic-based prejudice against him.

On the next trip to Theresa's to pick up Bobby, Steve encountered Raul outside again. Carmen was late delivering the child so the two sat down for a chat.

Both men had worked to restore good relations during the years that had passed since the previous custody fight, and neither wanted to return to the old hostilities.

"Look," Steve said, "I've contacted the Mediation Unit of the Court and asked them to set up an appointment for Carmen and me. Do you think she'll attend, or do you think she wants a knock-down-drag-out war again?"

"You know these women when they get religion in them," Raul said with a laugh. "Look at my wife and what a fanatic she is! I don't know, but I wouldn't be too hopeful if I were you."

"I'll be filing my own pleadings initially," Steve said. "You know how I feel about lawyers."

"How's that?" asked Raul.

"Well, for starters I almost agree with what Shakespeare had to say: 'The first thing we must do is kill all the lawyers!'" Steve chuckled. "Look, that last battle got pretty nasty, and I did some things to hurt your family that I wouldn't want to do again. I don't want this affair to go down like the last."

Raul was relieved to hear him talk that way, and he

promised Steve that he would not get involved this time. Carmen had moved in with her boyfriend and was, so far as he was concerned, living in sin. She would have to handle this one on her own. The two men shook hands on the agreement and separated just as Carmen drove up with Bobby.

Steve knew now that he was in good shape. If Carmen refused to go to the mediator, it would again be to his credit that he had tried to reconcile the differences while she refused to budge. If Carmen's family wouldn't back her, he could make more out of the fact that she was living out of wedlock with Ricardo. Now the father was the one who had the stable home life to offer Bobby. He was married. Carmen was only shacking up, and there were no kids for Bobby to play with anymore as there were when the boy was living at Theresa's. Carmen had also just quit her job with the airline. Steve knew she would argue that she was home more now to take care of Bobby. He also knew that Schmidt was very expensive. Robinson's strategy was to go it alone for as long as he could without hiring an attorney, try to drain Carmen and Ricardo of as much cash as possible through Schmidt's bills, and then hire an attorney for his side only when the trial itself was about to begin just to be sure that he had the proper mouthpiece and would not be seen as a "nut," which is how judges often perceive those who never hire a lawyer.

Sure enough, Carmen refused to attend the mediation session. Steve rationalized that he didn't care. She had to pay her attorney to notify me of her decision, he thought. The mediator was sympathetic enough to Steve to tell him how to phrase his initial petitions to the court. There were three that he filed: a "Petition to Enforce the Original Agreement Regarding Religious Upbringing of the Minor," one for "Modification of Visitation Rights," and one for "Modification of Final Judgment."

When Steve had finished typing these, he had a tremendous feeling of pride for he knew that they were good enough to get the ball rolling, and he also knew that he had just saved himself not less than five hundred dollars. He drove down to the courthouse to file them, mailed a copy to Schmidt, and hand-delivered another to Carmen, who had told Bobby that his father was not smart enough to do the job on his own.

Steve couldn't sleep that night. Like a chess player trying to guess his opponent's next move, his mind kept playing out a likely sequence of events that would follow. Carmen would probably run right over to Schmidt, wanting to know if the packet that he had given to her was any good. Schmidt would likely tell her at first that it was, but not to worry. He would take care of this "novice" without any difficulty.

The attorney would want to see any material that she might have which could be used as evidence. What would she give him? The letters that Steve had written to her? A copy of his book? Yes, both seemed likely.

The thought of a hostile attorney leafing through *The Great Christ Debate* gave Steve pleasure. He could picture Schmidt thinking, *This guy might not be as easy to shake off as I had first suspected. Any man who could finish writing a work of such magnitude would surely have the intelligence needed to keep firing legal papers at us.* Schmidt would probably tell Carmen that he would hire an attorney eventually. He'd be right, Steve knew.

The opposition would discuss citing the list of verses that he had given to Carmen. What would Schmidt's advice be? He needed something to build a case on. But to include the verses would mean that the attorney would have to argue that Steve had no right to teach Bobby about the Bible. That could turn the case into something that the Supreme Court might be interested in one day . . . the kind of case that could be worth lots of money and prestige for an attorney. It would give Steve publicity, too . . . something quite useful for an author, but something that would also be good for increasing his own level of stress and Bobby's, too. Not so good.

Steve assumed that Carmen would want to include the verses in her case (and it turned out that he was right. Her attorney used the material to try to show that Steve was poisoning Bobby's mind).

What, Steve worried, would Carmen tell Schmidt about the circumcision? She might insist that, although she was present, the whole ritual was conducted in Hebrew. Much of it was, but not all. Cantor Lipson had explained everything to her in English. She'd probably stress what was common knowledge about being born Jewish or non-Jewish . . . our law says its the mother that counts, not the father. God, that's gonna be a tough one to argue around. Some Reform rabbis want to modify the law so that if either parent is Jewish, the child can be so recognized, but they really haven't gotten anywhere with the idea yet, and I doubt that they ever will, he thought.

Schmidt would want to know about Bobby leading services at the Homestead Jewish Center. She would tell him the truth about that one. She knew that he was going to synagogue, but had not known about the boy's leadership until she read about it in the Petition, he knew. That's got to make her angry, he thought. She could argue that the six-year-old posing as her son was really a complete stranger. If so, she'd be certain to play up the alienation angle.

What would the lawyer tell her to do about Bobby's lack of a baptism? I stressed that in my Petition, Steve again worried. I told Bobby to never let anyone pour water on his head, but can he stop it if they try? What will Schmidt advise? If he's smart, he'll caution her not to do anything radical, but he could tell her that once it's done it will be a fait accompli! They could say that I tricked her into the circumcision when Bobby was too young to have a say in his destiny. Why couldn't she, as primary residential parent, return the favor? *Questions, Questions, Questions.* God, a man could go nuts from thinking about all this, he thought.

Time would show that the fruits of the meeting envisioned by Steve would include the necessary counter-petitions along with a "Petition to Terminate Joint Custody" and another to restrict visitation rights. Schmidt must have known the former petition would fall on deaf ears. He probably suspected that the latter would fare no better either. But like a quarterback attempting to throw a "Hail Mary" touchdown pass, he had a responsibility to mount the best offense possible for his client, and he wasn't about to let Steve rest for even a moment if he could help it.

Something else probably came from Carmen's meeting with Schmidt that day. The attorney must have recommended that a psychologist be put on the case to do an evaluation of Bobby. It seems likely that Carmen, fully aware of Bobby's sentiments, would have hesitated in going along with the idea. Yet from what followed, it is apparent that she must have reluctantly consented. Schmidt was undoubtedly "fishing" for material to use, and he could have argued that an unfavorable report could always be kept their own little secret. Besides, a good report would help him understand the dynamics of the case that he was about to take on. If Bobby's mind was being poisoned by Steve, the psychologist would certainly uncover evidence of it. That could make all the difference in the world.

Schmidt's initial strategy involved hitting his opponent with a blistering legal attack. He knew that the best defense is a strong offense. The documents that his office spit out at Robinson were designed to keep the school teacher's head spinning, to push him into the financial burden of hiring an attorney early in the battle. But if he spent any serious time studying Steve's book and the verse list that Carmen had brought in, he should have known that Steve was not a man to be frightened easily. Any man who will sell his house or give up a wife for a cause is a dangerous adversary. Robinson was a man who would choose death before turning his son over to the Pope.

— 9 —
THE BAPTISM

There was nothing in the short run that either Steve or his son could do about Carmen's desire to send Bobby to catechism class. Of course, Bobby did his best to make his presence known to the teacher, Mrs. Divine. On the first day there, the boy stood up and announced, "I'm a Jew. I don't belong here." But all the teacher had to say in return was, "Sit down; sometimes children don't know what they're saying. Your mother knows best."

The instructor did, of course, report the incident to the office where a record was started on little Bobby to see whether the remark was a fluke or something symptomatic of a greater problem. Carmen had not initially clued St. Mark's in on Bobby's past.

They began to suspect that something was really wrong when Bobby began to spout off many of the 24 verses that Steve had threatened to teach.

"Isn't it true," Bobby asked, "that Jesus said salvation is from the Jews? He said it in John 4:22, didn't he?" A teacher of six- and seven-year-olds normally doesn't get too many questions like that, and in short order Mrs. Divine found that she had a weekly theological war on her hands as Steve continued to grill the boy on how to destroy her class. One office-recorded remark quickly grew into a small book. Soon the teacher refused to take Bobby into her class unless Carmen sat in with him. That seemed to help, but what Mrs. Divine didn't realize was that Bobby was only being silenced now by beatings at home for his theological commentary.

Carmen knew that her son could not be baptized at St. Mark's for they had by now no doubts about Bobby's convictions. Still, she wasn't about to be stopped by opposition there, so she set out for the Church of the Holy Ascension.

Father Murray was Ascension's head priest. A 37-year-old, heavyset man, Murray had overseen his church's rise to be one of the largest congregations in Miami. He was proud of his accomplishment, but knew that the key to continued success was in good fund-raising techniques.

The following scenario is constructed from answers given to a later set of interogatories.

Carmen came to see the Father with Ricardo and checkbook in hand. She told him that she was anxious to see her son baptized as soon as possible.

"How old is the young man?" Murray asked.

"Six," Carmen said. Bobby was still five weeks short of his seventh birthday.

"And has he been instructed in the faith?" the priest asked.

"Oh, yes," Carmen said. "He's been attending catechism class at St. Mark's."

"Would you be the boy's father?" Murray asked of Ricardo.

"No, I'm Carmen's fiance'," he answered.

Carmen went on to explain that she was divorced from a Jew who was Bobby's father. Murray wanted to know how Carmen had been married to Steve. When he heard that the ceremony was performed by a notary, he was satisfied that she was free to marry Ricardo in the Church for this was, in the eyes of Catholicism, to be her first marriage.

"Did your son have a brith?" the Father asked.

"What's that?" Carmen asked innocently.

"A ritual circumcision," Murray informed her.

"Oh, Bobby's been circumcised. Is that a problem?" she asked.

"Not really. Even our Lord was circumcised. How soon do you want the baptism performed?" he wanted to know.

"Would tomorrow be too soon?" Carmen asked a bit nervously.

"Normally we require a child to attend our catechism class for three months, but the boy's under seven so he isn't yet quite at the age of consent," the Father said pensively.

"Would a large donation help?" Ricardo asked as he handed the priest a check.

"It would indeed," Murray beamed. "We'd be happy to accommodate you."

The following day Carmen dressed up Bobby in his new suit. Ricardo drove both to Ascension. Bobby sensed that something was different about this trip, and Carmen told the boy that the priest would "place a shield over his head to keep him from going to hell."

Steve had warned his son to never allow anyone in church to pour water over his head, but that was months ago and Bobby was too busy playing with a new toy in the car to give the upcoming event much thought.

In church Murray met privately with the couple while Bobby waited in the sanctuary. Ricardo told the priest that there would be no other relatives present that day because Carmen's parents were sick. Murray said that was O.K., called in two office workers to serve as witnesses, and then went out to do his duty.

The service was performed, at Carmen's request, mostly in Latin. Bobby had no idea what was happening until he saw that the priest was sprinkling him with water. By then it was too late.

In the car on the way home, Ricardo laughed at the boy. "Well, Bobby, you're one of us now!" he taunted. Carmen held up the baptism certificate for her son to see. "Now you're Catholic, too," she boasted.

Bobby started to cry. He thought that his father would kill him or worse, that his father wouldn't love him anymore. The next few days were pure agony for the former pride of the Homestead Jewish Center.

On Wednesday Carmen drove her son to her mother's house about an hour before Steve came over to pick him up for the first time since the baptism occurred. Carmen told her mother what she had done, expecting Theresa to be happy. After all, it had been her mother who initially started the fight with Steve over the baptism issue. The end result of that feud was the divorce.

Carmen was shocked to learn that her mother was furious about what she had done.

"Bobby's more of a Jew than his father is!" Theresa shouted. "I've tried to win the boy for Christ for years now. He wouldn't have any of it! You can't make him a Christian by just sprinkling water over his head!"

"I can and I did," Carmen snapped back. "His father said in his petition to the court that Bobby was never baptized. Well, that's not true anymore, is it? His old man also complained about me living out of wedlock. I'll take care of that, too. Just wait, you'll see. Ricardo loves me. He's paying my bills, and he promised to marry me," Carmen said emphatically.

Theresa looked at the boy. Bobby was crying again, and she felt that her daughter had violated his rights as a human being. "Don't worry," Theresa told him. "You're still a Jew, Bobby. Jesus was a Jew. His disciples were Jews. We're all Jews. Now you're a *complete* Jew, too."

At that moment, Bobby heard his father honk the horn. He ran out of the door with tears still under his eyes, but with a smile on his lips.

"Hi, Daddy! Guess what just happened! It's great. Grandma says I can be a *complete* Jew. She says Jesus was a Jew, and we're all Jews!"

"What in the world are you talking about?" Steve asked. "That doesn't sound at all like the Theresa I know!" He was especially wary about the *complete Jew* phrase. Christians often used the term to refer to Jews that they had won over. To Jews it made about as much sense as the Vietnam War phrase "We had to destroy a village to save it."

Bobby let the truth out. "Mommy had me baptized but Grandma says it doesn't count. I'm still Jewish!"

Steve wanted to die. "My God!" he exclaimed, "You aren't a Jew anymore! I told you to never let them pour water on your head!"

"I'm sorry," Bobby said choking in tears. "I forgot."

Bobby went on to tell his father about how he had been tricked into the baptism. His father was a turmoil of mixed emotions. He felt rage at Carmen, more at her priest and the Church he represented, and deep disappointment in his son.

For the next five hours Steve remained in a rage, refusing to comfort his son. At home he even broke Bobby's toy Israeli F-16. The plane had been the boy's favorite toy, for it had his Hebrew name, Moshe, stenciled on it. Bobby's most precious possession had been his Jewish identity. Now it lay shattered with the F-16 on the floor of his room.

At last the father knew what he had to do. He felt terrible about the way he had behaved. No one, not even the pope himself, could destroy the love that he had for his son. He walked into Bobby's room, gave him a big hug, and asked him to forgive him for acting that way. Then he promised to sue the Church right up to the Pope himself.

"What about my F-16?" Bobby wanted to know.

"I'll build you another. But first, you're gonna have to earn it. The men who fly that plane all lay their lives on the line for our people. When I know that you're of the same mind, you'll have it. Not before," Steve promised.

The following day Steve called the Archdiocese of Miami to inform them that he would sue for six million dollars unless they annulled the baptism. He also called the Jewish Federation and the *Miami Herald* to give them the news. On the same day he received Schmidt's counter-petitions. They were 39 pages long.

— 10 —
A MATTER OF SPIRITUAL CUSTODY

Most of Schmidt's 39 pages were pure hogwash, easy for Steve to counter in his Answers to the Counter-petitions. Much of what Steve had alleged in his original Petitions he could back with documentation. Schmidt had made the mistake of denying almost everything, and now it was Steve's turn to prove the attorney wrong. Steve's Answers were one hundred pages long with about one-third of that bulk being verbiage and the rest documentation.

Schmidt had alleged that Steve intended to run off to Israel, but Steve produced a copy of his Coast Guard enlistment contract which still had another five years remaining. That proved he had no intention of going anywhere.

The attorney denied the religious nature of the circumcision, and Steve submitted a copy of the brith milah certificate to prove otherwise.

Schmidt only admitted to two of Steve's assertions: that Bobby had been circumcised and that the boy saw himself as being Jewish. Much of Schmidt's work was inconsistent. For example, he argued that Bobby enjoyed catechism class but then claimed the boy always refused to go to it because his father had brainwashed him. He said Bobby loved his mother, but that the father had alienated the child's affection for her.

Steve took about two weeks to complete his response. The complaint in such an action would normally be against the mother alone, but Steve went on to argue that the Catholic Church itself was not an appropriate institution for anyone with Jewish blood to follow. He then began to document the Vatican's anti-Semitic history, a dangerous tact to take, he knew, but a necessary one. His case was to be a matter of spiritual custody, based around his belief that the Church's hands were too bloody to merit gaining the soul of even a half Jew, as Bobby was.

What was it that the Catholic judge would now be forced to read? The attack on Rome started with an account of Vatican-sponsored persecution of the Jews right back to Pope Urban II, who raised the first Crusader army which had slaughtered about 10,000 Jews in the year 1096. Then he spoke of Torquemada and the Spanish Inquisition of 1492, and of Pope Pius V who (in 1569) expelled the Jews from all States of the Church, except Rome and Ancona for commercial reasons. He listed the failure of the Church to come to the aid of Jews killed during the Chmielnicki massacres of 1648 in which more than 100,000 Jews died, and the fact that in Rome Pope Pius X maintained the Jewish Ghetto until 1870. Then, and only then, did he begin to document the Vatican's role in the Nazi-led Holocaust.

Robinson had managed to travel back in time to 1933 with the help of the microfilm library at Florida International University. There, in copies of the *New York Times*, he found all the evidence that he would need to prove his point.

Steve argued that the Vatican entered into a Concordat with the Hitler government on July 20, 1933, after speeches had already been made in the U.S. Senate quoting Hitler's suggestion that 12,000 to 15,000 Jews be held under poison gas. The first *Times* article about the Senate speech was on pages 1 and 25 of the June 11, 1933, issue.

When the *New York Times* covered the signing of the Vatican-Nazi pact on page 5 of its July 21st, 1933, issue, he showed that the story was only three columns to the left of an article called "*World Jews Push Boycott Of Reich For 'Inhuman' Acts.*" The article said back on page 1 that the Hitler government had "expressed its determination to persist in its policy of persecution and to drive the Jews of Germany from every branch of activity in public and private life, to annihilate them economically, to deprive them of their citizenship, to reduce them to a state of pariahs and eventually to *EXTERMINATE* them." It listed, on its page 5 continuance, the fact that "hundreds of thousands of unoffending Jews have been imprisoned, tortured and lodged in hells on earth, called detention camps." Thus, Steve argued, it was common knowledge that the concentration camps existed and that Hitler wanted to kill all the Jews when the Vatican signed the agreement. He quoted *The Rise And Fall Of The Third Reich* (page 324) by William L. Shirer, who said that the Concordat, " . . . signed by Papal Secretary of State, Monsignor Pacelli, later Pope Pius XII," came " . . . at a moment when the first excesses of the new regime in Germany had provoked worldwide revulsion" and that "the Concordat undoubtedly lent the Hitler government much badly needed prestige."

An article in section II on page 4 of the *New York Times* September 10, 1933, issue showed that the Pope was aware of the plight of the Jews. It read, "The report that ratification of the Vatican-German concordat has been delayed by the Pope's dissatisfaction with Chancellor Hitler's policies, especially sterilization and anti-Judaism is denied by both the Vatican and by German sources." Two days later, in the September 12th issue, the *Times* reported on page 10 that the Concordat had been ratified. This article stated, "Nazi newspapers view the ratification as new proof of the stability of political conditions in Germany since Adolf Hitler took over the government and as a rebuke to foreign meddling. Less than twenty-four hours ago, the Nazis assert those meddlers proclaimed that the pact would be doomed by Papal veto."

The most damning piece of evidence introduced on the topic, however, was a photocopy of page 10 from the December 16, 1933, issue of the *Times*:

PARLEYS ON JEWS
DENIED BY VATICAN

> Report of Negotiations With Reich on Status of Those Who Are Catholics Is Refuted.
>
> ROME, Dec. 15. — The Vatican denies that any negotiations are in process with the German Government concerning the status and treatment of Catholics of Jewish blood.
>
> *It is pointed out that The Vatican could intervene on behalf of this class of German citizens only if they were being subjected to unfair*

treatment as a consequence of being Catholics. Since this is not the case, the whole matter is regarded as being purely an internal German affair.

The only other case, it is stated, in which The Vatican might consider itself called on to intervene would be if Catholic priests were being prevented from carrying out their duties because of Jewish descent. Only two such cases have been brought to the notice of the ecclesiastical authorities, but the Vatican did not consider it advisable to join issue with the German Government on the strength of only two such cases, and let the matter drop.

JUNE 1933

VOL. LXXXII....No. 27,532.

NAZI JEWISH POLICY ASSAILED IN SENATE AS PERIL TO PEACE

Robinson, Democratic Leader, Attacks the 'Persecution' as 'Sickening and Terrifying.'

WARNS AS TO PENALTIES

Forecasts Loss of Trade and Prestige and a Reaction Among German People.

...TTACK

inu..
appears ..
driving Jews ..
tions and of deny...
opportunity to earn their ..

Hitler's Statements Quoted.

As early as 1924, Chancellor Hitler wrote a book entitled "My Struggle." The twelfth edition was printed in Munich in 1932 and is alleged to declare at page 70:

"If the Jew wins * * * his crown of victory is the death wreath of humanity, and this planet will once again, as it did ages ago, float through the ether bereft of men. * * * When I defend myself against the Jews, I fight for the work of the Lord."

At Page 344, it is asserted:

"If, at the beginning of the war, 12,000 or 15,000 of these corruptors of the people had been held under poison gas, just as hundreds of thousands of our very best German workmen * * * had to bear it in the field, then the sacrifice of millions at the front would not have been in vain. On the contrary, 12,000 scoundrels removed at the right time might perhaps have saved the lives of 1,000,000 proper Germans of value for the future."

Je..
outlawed ..
all contracts w..
cotts of Jewish drugg..
opticians, dentists and X-r..
stitutes are prompted and encouraged.

Ban by the Universities.

Universities are closed to Jewish scientists and students. The right of Jewish children to attend primary schools is limited or denied.

Almost every profession and vocation is closed against persons of Jewish blood. This astounding and oppressive policy is rendered the more intolerable by decrees forbidding Jews to leave Germany.

Nazi songs sung at parades and mass meetings stimulate and crystallize the spirit of anti-Semitism. It is sufficient to quote two stanzas:

The Fatherland needs men,
It is in dreadful plight.
It is only when Jews die
That German suffering ends.

Thus do the storm columns
Stand ready for the battle of the races.
It is only when Jews bleed
That we are liberated.

Pages 1 and 25
Special to *The New York Times*
Printed June 11, 1933

Second-Class Matter,
New York, N. Y.

NEW YORK, FRIDAY, JULY 21, 1933.

WORLD JEWS PUSH BOYCOTT OF REICH FOR 'INHUMAN' ACTS

Amsterdam Session Calls on All People, Regardless of Race, to Join Movement.

WIDE EFFECTS REPORTED

Sharp Cuts in German Exports Are Noted Especially in Holland and Egypt.

By FREDERICK T. BIRCHALL.

Wireless to THE NEW YORK TIMES,

AMSTERDAM, July 20.—In this city upon free Dutch soil where, almost 400 years ago Jews driven from Spain and Portugal found a safe refuge, establishing a colony which in the next generation produced the great philosopher, Spinoza, some thirty representatives of world Jewry met today to deal with Germany's modern revival of Jewish persecution.

They elected Samuel Untermyer of New York president and adopted this resolution:

Whereas the Jews of Germany have for centuries been imbedded in its soil and at all times have been and are loyal, useful and law-abiding citizens who have freely sacrificed their lives for their fatherland in times of war and have contributed to its prosperity and won world-wide distinction in all the arts and sciences and in literature and the professions, manifestly out of proportion to population and

Whereas world opinion and the unanimous outcry, protests and demonstrations of Jews and non-Jews throughout the civilized world against the incredibly inhuman policy of the Hitler government toward the Jews of Germany have been unavailing; and

Whereas the Hitler government has repeatedly expressed its determination to persist in its policy of persecution and to drive the Jews of Germany from every branch of activity in public and private life, to annihilate them economically, to deprive them of their citizenship, to reduce them to the state of pariahs and eventually to exterminate them; and

Whereas Germany under the leadership of the Nazi government has established and is con-

THE NEW YORK TIMES, FRIDAY, JULY 21, 1933

EDDY ASSAILS NAZIS AT BERLIN MEETING

American Sociologist Tells His Amazed Hearers No Nation Can Flout World Opinion.

STRESSES REACTION HERE

Scores Treatment of Jews, Socialists and Liberals and Denial of Liberty.

Wireless to THE NEW YORK TIMES.

BERLIN, July 20.—Sherwood Eddy, American sociologist, dumbfounded a representative gathering of German officials and leaders of business and the professions here today by declaring that American opinion was becoming increasingly apprehensive over some of the things happening in the Nazi Germany.

He deplored the new German attitude toward liberalism and racial problems and asserted that no country could afford to flout world opinion. The world, he believed, had a right to know how the new Germany intended to justify its treatment of the Jews, liberals and Socialists.

Mr. Eddy, former secretary for Asia of the Y. M. C. A. and leader of the traveling American Seminar, a group of well-known educators and professional men now making

Nazi Church Law Held Inapplicable in Saar

By The Associated Press.

SAARBRUECKEN, Saar Basin, July 20.—Organization of Chancellor Hitler's Nazi church as the official faith was barred in this territory today by the League of Nations governing commission.

The Nazi church law was declared inapplicable because the people must be religiously and politically free until 1935, when a plebiscite is to determine whether the Saar Basin will be attached to France or Germany.

REICH CONCORDAT SIGNED AT VATICAN

Papen and Cardinal Pacelli Put Signatures on Accord and Text Will Be Issued Today.

GERMAN HAILS AGREEMENT

Declares It Guarantees Beneficial Cooperation Between Church and State for First Time.

VATICAN CITY, July 20 (AP).—The concordat between Germany and the Vatican was signed today by Vice Chancellor Franz von Papen and Cardinal Pacelli, the Papal Secretary of State.

KREISLER IS FIRM ON REICH CONCERTS

Says He Will Refuse to Appear Until Deeds Follow Pledge of Artistic Freedom.

RECEIVES MANY OFFERS

But Rejects Them Till Musicians Are Not Only Tolerated but Welcome, Regardless of Faith.

By The Associated Press.

BERLIN, July 20.—Fritz Kreisler, the violinist, said today that he would continue to refuse to appear in Germany despite the announcement by Hans Hinkel, Prussian State Commissioner for Culture, that in Hitlerite Germany "the free artistic activities of foreigners and non-Aryans [Jews] shall in nowise be hindered."

Mr. Kreisler, who since his return from the United States has been flooded with requests to appear in concerts here, said he would wait until these words of the commissioner were followed by deeds.

"I appreciate Commissioner Hinkel's announcement, but before I appear I must see it established beyond peradventure of doubt that all my colleagues in the musical world, irrespective of nationality, race or creed, are not only tolerated but actually welcomed," he declared.

"My friend Furtwaengler [Dr. Wilhelm Furtwaengler, conductor

WORLD JEWS PUSH BOYCOTT OF REICH

By FREDERICK T. BIRCHALL.

Continued from Page One.

the United States, Britain and France and including such distant lands as South Africa and Egypt and such close neighbors to Germany as Holland, Belgium and Poland, and even little Latvia, had delegates at the table at the Carlton Hotel, around which the thirty sat.

Allied Jewish organizations in ten other countries wrote or telegraphed that, although unable to send representatives, they would endorse and loyally support any action the conference might see fit to take.

The delegates were grimly determined and businesslike. They began by appointing three committees of three members each. These comprise: The committee on resolutions, composed of the delegates from France, Poland and Czechoslovakia; the committee on organization, manned by the delegates from Holland, Egypt and America, and the committee on finance, with the delegates from Britain, Belgium and Lithuania.

Reports were read and referred, outlining the steps already taken and the progress made in the prosecution of the boycott in the various countries. They showed serious inroads had been made already upon Germany's trade with the rest of the world.

cold and merciless campaign of persecution against 600,000 German Jews in the country which was once Germany, but is now more appropriately dubbed Hitlerland, furnished the first supreme test of the League of Nations.

League Is Criticised.

"To the supreme disappointment of its friends the League has not lifted its hand to stay this catastrophe that has been inflicted by one of its most important members upon a great army of its own defenseless citizens.

"Unless the League now moves quickly and before this world tragedy, being enacted day by day before our horror-stricken eyes, is complete, it might as well fold its tents and slink away, for its impotence and uselessness to deal with great issues of humanity will have been demonstrated.

"Here are some of the things the League can and should at once do if it is to justify its existence:

1. Send a select committee into Hitlerland to investigate and report fully upon the facts, and especially upon the pretexts whereon hundreds of thousands of unoffending German Jews have been imprisoned, tortured and lodged in hells on earth, called detention camps.

Nansen Passports Are Urged.

2. Provide Nansen passports for those able to leave Germany, which would permit them to take their property with them, as was done by the League in the cases of Russia, Greece and Rumania, and thus open to them the gates of foreign lands.

4. Enforce the labor union provisions of the Versailles Treaty, which are being flagrantly violated by the expulsion and exclusion

PARLEYS ON JEWS DENIED BY VATICAN

Report of Negotiations With Reich on Status of Those Who Are Catholics Is Refuted.

Wireless to THE NEW YORK TIMES.

ROME, Dec. 15.—The Vatican denies that any negotiations are in progress with the German Government concerning the status and treatment of Catholics of Jewish blood.

It is pointed out that the Vatican could intervene on behalf of this class of German citizens only if they were being subjected to unfair treatment as a consequence of being Catholics. Since this is not the case, the whole matter is regarded as being purely an internal German affair.

The only other case, it is stated, in which the Vatican might consider itself called on to intervene would be if Catholic priests were being prevented from carrying out their duties because of their Jewish descent. Only two such cases have been brought to the notice of the ecclesiastical authorities, but the Vatican did not consider it advisable to join issue with the German Government on the strength of only two such cases, and let the matter drop.

It is also denied that any negotiations are in progress between the Vatican and Germany concerning the intention of the German Government to exclude the Old Testament or a part of it from the curricula of the schools.

Page 10
New York Times
December 16, 1933

CONCORDAT DELAY DENIED.

Pope's Disapproval of Nazi Policies Not Holding Up Ratification.

Wireless to THE NEW YORK TIMES.

ROME, Sept. 9.—The report that the ratification of the Vatican-German concordat has been delayed by the Pope's dissatisfaction with Chancellor Hitler's policies, especially sterilization and anti-Judaism, is denied both by the Vatican and by German sources.

Admittedly, the Vatican does not approve several of the Nazi policies, but this condition existed before the conclusion of the concordat and has become no worse since.

The concordat with Austria, concluded six weeks before that with Germany, is still unratified. Cardinal Pacelli, Papal Secretary of State, is about to leave for Switzerland for a vacation. It is expected the ratification will follow soon after his return.

Section II, Page 4
New York Times
September 10, 1933

VATICAN AND REICH RATIFY CONCORDAT

Church Agrees to Refrain From Political Activity—State Permits Catholic Associations.

VATICAN CITY, Sept. 11 (AP).—The concordat between Germany and the Holy See, agreed upon in July, was ratified yesterday. The final text arrived from Berlin by airplane and formal ratifications were exchanged by Cardinal Pacelli, the Papal Secretary of State, and Dr. Eugene von Klee, counselor in the German Embassy here.

The Osservatore Romano, official organ of the Holy See, published the following communiqué:

"Prior to the interchange his Holiness sent to the government of the Reich a series of points concerning interpretation of the concordat and those portions in which it has already been in effect. These are connected with the existence, activity and protection of Catholic organizations and the liberty of German Catholics to expound and explain publicly and in the Catholic press the doctrines and maxims of Catholic faith and morality.

"The government of the Reich has declared its readiness to treat with the aforesaid material in the near future."

The concordat combines the substance of separate accords previously entered into with the States of Prussia, Baden and Bavaria. By its terms the church agreed to refrain from interference in political affairs. The State promised to permit functions of lay and clerical Catholic associations provided they confine themselves to religious activities.

Germans Gratified.

Special Cable to THE NEW YORK TIMES.

BERLIN, Sept. 11.—The ratification of the concordat between the Reich and the Vatican was welcomed with relief by the German press today. The gratification appears all the more pronounced because the action coincides with the German Catholic Congress in Vienna.

Nazi newspapers view the ratification as new proof of the stability of political conditions in Germany since Adolf Hitler took over the government and as a rebuke to foreign meddling. Less than twenty-four hours ago, the Nazis assert, those meddlers proclaimed that the pact would be doomed by a Papal veto.

Page 10
New York Times
September 12, 1933

Steve pointed out that any Church which could imply its approval to kill or persecute its own members so long as it was because of their Jewish ancestry and not because of their present faith had no right to lay its hands on his half-Jewish son. He noted that the Vatican had proven that it would not even stand up for its own priests if they had Jewish parents or grandparents (under Nazi law anyone with one Jewish grandparent was classified as a Jew for extermination purposes).

Having done his homework, Steve invited Fred Strasser, reporter for the *Miami Herald*, over for dinner. Steve was not the only one who believed in doing a thorough job. By the time he had arrived, Fred had been down to the courthouse to read the entire case file and even a good part of *The Great Christ Debate*, which was sitting there as evidence from the previous trial.

Fred's first question was about the book. He wanted to know if Robinson still stood by his earlier positive views of Jesus as a legitimate prophet. "No," Steve told him. "There were too many unfulfilled prophecies." He then proceeded to give him a history of the discord that faith in Jesus had brought to his family.

Steve had two main interests in giving the *Herald* the story. He didn't want to get "railroaded" as he felt he had been before, and he wanted to warn other Jews and Christians as to the dangers that existed in interfaith marriages. Seventy percent of all marriages between Jews and Christians end in divorce. Steve wanted others to know about the kind of heartache that awaited many who chose to repeat his mistake.

The hardest thing for the father to talk about was the

fact that Carmen had tricked his son into the baptism. Fred wanted to ask Bobby about that himself. The boy was there that night, and Bobby gave him the full run down. Fred asked him why he didn't want to be Christian or go to church with his mother. Bobby told him, "I don't want to go to church because Jesus was a false prophet."

Fred asked him why he thought that was so. The lad responded, almost parrot-like that, there were three reasons for his belief. "First," the boy said, "the Messiah is supposed to bring peace, and Jesus said he came to bring war. Second, everything a true prophet predicts must come true, and some of Jesus' predictions like a quick return didn't come true. And third . . . third . . . I can't remember the third reason, but it's a good one," he told Strasser.

The reporter laughed and congratulated Steve on the excellent conditioning job.

"I know," Robinson admitted, "that it appears the boy's been brainwashed, but the truth is that he's been raised one way from birth . . . Jewish. That was what his mother agreed to and I have the documentation I need to prove it in a court of law."

Fred grilled him on a number of other issues, including the charges that Carmen had made in her pleadings during the past and present court cases. He was particularly concerned about Carmen's allegations of financial irresponsibility. Steve began to feel as if he were on the witness stand as Fred did his very best to ensure a fair and impartial story. He asked for Carmen's phone number, too, but Carmen refused to talk to him when he called. She remembered Schmidt's warning about Steve's desire for publicity, and she wanted to take no part in aiding him.

Fred told Steve that he would probably print the story in about a week or two, thanked him for the dinner, and left after spending about two hours taking notes.

The following day Rabbi Goldin from the Jewish Federation called to say that he had arranged a meeting with Archbishop McCarthy to discuss a possible settlement. Steve was elated. Now he was getting somewhere.

The conference was set for a Friday afternoon. Steve had just put the finishing touches on all his Answers to Schmidt's Counter-Petitions, so he decided to file them at the courthouse on the way to the meeting at the Federation. He knew that the Archdiocese would have a high-powered legal firm working for it, and he hoped that the Church's attorney would find the Holocaust materials in the court file. He knew that it would be better for them to discover the exhibits on their own than for him to tell them about it. That way they'd fear him more.

It wasn't an easy day to drive around town. There was a civil disturbance in Liberty City, not far from the Federation Building, and many of the roads were cordoned off by the police. This caused him to be late for his meeting by about fifteen minutes. He didn't want to keep the archbishop waiting, but nervously rationalized that the Vatican had kept his people waiting for humane treatment for almost a thousand years.

When he arrived at the office with his wife, he suddenly realized that he hadn't really thought much about how to behave. After all, how often does a Jew tell an archbishop that he's ready to sue the Vatican for six million bucks unless Rome goes into the business of annulling baptisms?

Robinson soon learned he hadn't been keeping an archbishop waiting at all, for it was not McCarthy that was with the rabbi, but Monsignor Walsh, the man in charge of community relations for the Archdiocese of Miami. Steve shook the rabbi's hand and then Walsh's. There was a long moment of silence as each man looked at the other and waited for him to start. As Steve sat there waiting, visions of the Inquisition and Holocaust ran through his mind, as did thoughts of Jacob Frank who, while claiming to be a reincarnation of Sabbatai Sevi, apostatized and converted to the Catholic religion. The man before him, Steve felt, was the enemy — a man who stood for much of what was wrong with the world. He decided to rip into him.

"I want to know where the hell your priest gets off baptizing my son Catholic?" With that, the irate parent got out of his seat, walked towards Walsh and started to lay papers down on the man's lap.

"This," Steve proclaimed, "is Bobby's circumcision certificate which states in Hebrew *Lishane Gerute* "for conversion purposes" providing that his mother consented to raise him as a Jew, and this, my dear friend, is a copy of her attorney's Answer to my Petition to Enforce the Original Religious Agreement regarding the Minor Child. Filed only four days *before* your priest baptized my son, it admits to the Court that Bobby sees himself as being Jewish!"

"How could the Father have known about this?" Walsh asked.

"He could have known about Bobby's beliefs by simply taking five minutes in private to talk to the boy. My son, like me, has a tongue, too."

"Calm down," the rabbi urged after letting Steve make his most important points. "The Monsignor is not your enemy. He's here to obtain the facts. The man knows almost nothing about the case. Please be polite!"

"Excuse me," Steve said, "I'm more than a bit upset by the whole thing. Do you see this book?" he asked, holding up a copy of *The Great Christ Debate*. "I spent nearly three years of my life writing it for my son's spiritual enlightenment." Opening the book, he continued, "That's Bobby's name on the dedication page. You'll notice that I even made certain that his Hebrew name was printed under his English one. If you can't read Hebrew, it says Moshe Ben Ithamar HaLevi; which means Moses, son of Ithamar the Levite. When a man writes a book for his son and then goes so far as to put the boy's Hebrew name on the dedication page, you can't expect him to be exactly overjoyed to learn that the Catholic Church has ignored the joint custody that he had fought hard in court to obtain, and against his will and the boy's, violated the constitutionally guaranteed right of freedom of religion for his son. You know, I've spent years researching your Church, and I'd just love to start a crusade against it and all it stands for!"

"I think *crusade* is, historically, more a word that belongs to the Monsignor than to us," Goldin chuckled.

"You're certainly right about that, rabbi," Steve agreed.

"You know, Monsignor, your Church burned Jews at the stake during the Spanish Inquisition because we refused to be baptized. This isn't Spain and I'm not gonna march quietly to the stake either."

The Monsignor denied that the Inquisition was the fault of the Church in Spain. "That was a government action," he said.

"You'd like us to think that, wouldn't you? I haven't

been able to find any record of Vatican opposition to it. If there's one thing that sickens me about the history of the Jews, it's how many times we stood there and let your Church walk over us. Well, I'm not gonna be herded like one of those kosher sheep to the slaughter. We won't tolerate that brand of Judaism again, Mister. My price is six million dollars in memory of the six million which your Vatican Concordat with Hitler helped kill . . . unless you give me something more important than money, the baptismal annulment and with it the return of the honor of my people. Somebody, somewhere, sometime has got to stand up to your organization and say *no*. I never did believe in a *Let George Do It* philosophy, so that somebody has got to be *me*, the place is *here*, and the time is *now*," Steve rested, feeling proud that he had not been afriad to let his true feelings out.

The Monsignor looked like someone had just slugged him with a two-by-four. He had been holding his head as though he were in some kind of pain. Finally, he answered.

"From what you've shown me," he sighed, "I believe a serious mistake has occurred. I don't think that the priest would have conducted the baptism had he known of all this. Do you mind if I take copies of the legal pleadings you've handed me? I'm especially interested in the mother's admission about Bobby's Jewish identity. Please believe me, we don't wish to harm the child psychologically. Our greatest fear is that this fight might so disturb the boy as to cause him to abandon all faith."

Steve handed the Monsignor copies of all the evidence while the rabbi reinforced Walsh's plea and pointed out that the Church had expressed a sincere desire to resolve the matter before the meeting had started.

"Can you annul it?" Steve asked.

"We'll do all in our power to accommodate you. We want to maintain good relations with the Jewish community. It will, however, take some time to give you a definitive answer. Remember, it takes six months to annul a marriage, and we do that all the time. From all I've been able to determine by searching the literature, we've never annulled a baptism in the nearly two thousand years that our Church has existed. There are some heavy doctrinal questions to be resolved before rendering a decision like that."

Steve told the clergymen that Fred Strasser of the *Miami Herald* had promised to print the story soon. Walsh was upset about that and asked Steve to please try to delay publication. Goldin, too, argued that the story would not be good for community relations which were already strained by the rioting that day.

"The rabbi," Robinson said, "is being diplomatic. That's his job, not mine. I'll do what I can with the *Herald* but you must understand the decision to print is now in their hands, not mine. As for giving your Church time to make a proper determination, I don't have the luxury of waiting forever. My suit will be filed against Rome when the status of the custody battle dictates that kind of action. The baptism must be annulled *before* a judge renders a decision on custody. If I see that you can't get me the letter I want by then, I will file. That's a promise." The meeting then broke up.

— 11 —
WHAT'S IN A NAME

On Sunday, March 18, 1984, the phone rang early waking up Steve. It was his mother calling.

"Well, you've achieved fame around this town," she said.

Still half asleep, Steve asked her what she was talking about.

"I started reading the *Herald* at breakfast and almost fell over when I saw Bobby's picture. There's a huge two-page story about the whole thing. It's called *Divorced Parents Fight For Spiritual Custody Of Son,*" she said.

"My God, I asked them to hold off on the story. What's it like?" Steve asked a bit nervously.

"Well, it's very unbiased. I guess it favors you, but only slightly. The writer managed to dig up Carmen's complaints about you from the pleadings, and he published them all. There's two pictures. Most of your concerns are there including the fact that Carmen agreed to the brith milah. The article quotes Bobby as saying, 'I don't want to go to church because Jesus is a false prophet,' and says you admitted that your son was baptized . . . here it is, Bobby said, 'Mommy said she was going to place a shield over my head so I wouldn't go to hell.'"

Steve thanked her for the call, got dressed, and rushed out to buy ten copies of the paper. In the car, the radio talk shows were full of gossip about the case which was the headline story of the local section in the *Herald*.

Steve read it and found the financial accusations to be more than annoying, especially because he had given Strasser material to refute all that Carmen had alleged. Then again, he worried more about how Carmen would treat their son when she read what he had to say about Jesus. One thing he was sure of. Bobby had earned a new Israeli F-16 and more. He had stood up to a Christian world and told them that their Messiah was not a Messiah at all. The proud father rushed to a toy store and quickly restored the boy's symbol of self-identity.

At work the next day, Dr. Levy, Assistant Principal, warned Steve to be careful about what he had to say in class. Already the hate calls were starting to come in. An article like that was more than what was needed to bring all the anti-Semites crawling out of the woodwork.

In class one of his students asked, "Do Jews believe in God?"

"We not only believe in God," he said, "but we gave you most of your Bible."

"Then why'd ya kill God on the cross?" another asked.

"Look," Steve answered, "Jews believe in God and a Messiah to come, but we don't think Jesus is either. And as for killing him, it was the Romans who did it."

"My parents think you're nuts for putting your kid through the stuff we read about in the paper," a third boy said.

As his eye tic returned, he ordered, "Let's get on with the lesson. Anyone who brings up this case in class again will get a conduct cut. Get your news from the paper, not from me."

Robinson began to read more about Sabbatai Sevi. "Do you know," he asked Ruth, "that you and I were married the same week as Sabbatai Sevi was married to his third wife, Sarah. We even left on our main honeymoon on the same day, April 1st. The more I read about the man, the more we seem to have in common. I wonder why Rabbi Shoulson named me Sabbatai. Even more important, I wonder if he believes in reincarnation."

"Where's Shoulson now?" Ruth asked.

"The last time I saw the man I was eight days old, and he had a knife in his hand. That was 37 years ago. I doubt the man's still alive. Who knows? If he is, he might still be in Philly," Steve guessed. Then he decided to call information to find out if there was any Rabbi Morris Shoulson listed in the Philadelphia phone book. To his surprise, there was.

"Are you going to call the man?" Ruth wanted to know.

"What would I say to him? He'd think I'm crazy for sure if I suggested I had thoughts about being Sevi," Steve said.

"If you don't call now while the rabbi's still alive, you'll always wonder what he would have said. You can't call him once he's dead, and he's got to be very old by now. Call him," Ruth suggested.

Steve felt like a fool as he dialed the phone again. The rabbi answered it; and after a brief conversation, it was clear that this indeed was the mohel who had circumcised and named him 37 years before. The rabbi said that he had, on occasion, given babies the name Sabbatai.

"Why are you so interested in your name?" the rabbi asked with an accent like that of Sir Lawrence Olivier when he played the old cantor in the movie *The Jazz Singer.*"

"This isn't easy for me to talk about," Steve told him. "Do you believe in *Tiqqun Neshama?*"

"You mean *Tiqqun Gilgoth* don't you?" Shoulson asked.

"Yes, you know . . . reincarnation," Steve asked sheepishly.

"The concept has its place in Jewish theology," stated the President of the Philadelphia Rabbinical Council.

"I know that," Steve said. "My question is do *you* believe in it?"

It took some time to draw an answer from the rabbi. Most leading Rabbis don't like to discuss mysticism over the phone with strangers, but Shoulson eventually acknowledged his belief in the "transmigration of souls." Having heard this, Steve decided to go ahead and let the rabbi know of the "similarities that he'd discovered."

"I'm interested in a man known as Sabbatai Sevi. I need not tell you about the disastrous consequences of his life. We seem to share much in common, including the Hebrew name that you chose to give me for some reason.

"Like Sevi, I practiced a combination of Judaism and Islam for a number of years. I've had dreams of Istanbul years before I learned that Sabbatai apostatized there, and I've never been to the city myself. Sevi was a false messiah, and my first book, *The Great Christ Debate*, attempted to reconcile the theological differences dividing Judaism, Christianity and Islam, something that's the kind of task only a true Messiah could succeed at. Sabbatai apostatized when the Sultan threatened to cut off his head, and I have a scar on my neck that makes people tell me it looks like someone tried to cut off my head. I share another scar in common with Sevi, one of unexplained origin that often made me wonder if you had, perhaps, a slip of the knife 37 years ago.

"Sevi was reputed to be a master kabbalist according to what I was told while studying at a yeshiva in Jerusalem. I've tried to do some kabbalistic meditation and had some very strange results.

"Sevi's third wife, Sarah, was like mine in many ways. Sarah was a maid in a hospice before he married her. Ruth, my third wife, was a maid in a hospital. Sarah was adopted by a Polish nobleman and raised Catholic. Ruth, a Korean, was adopted by a descendant of Polish nobility, Michael Harris, who is a Catholic. Sarah converted to Judaism as an adult. So did Ruth. Sarah had visions of marrying the Messiah and being a queen. Ruth always overdresses for everything as though she subconsciously thinks she's a queen. She even wears evening gowns to go to the drugstore!

"I'm fighting for custody of my son now, as Sabbatai once did for his boy, Ishmael Mordecai. Ishmael was eventually separated from his mother when the boy was seven. Sarah died then. If I win in court, my son, who's now seven, will be largely separated from his current mother at the same age, while Ruth, who may have been his mother before, may regain him in this life while he's the same age as he was when she lost him before. I don't know if I'm making any sense. I guess this sounds pretty ridiculous. I'm sorry I troubled you," Steve said, feeling like an idiot.

"I'd appreciate it if you'd write down all you've told me

tonight and send it to me in a letter so I may study the matter. Include a copy of your book. Tell me, if you were Sevi, why do you feel that you might have come back?" Shoulson asked.

"I'm not sure, but I'm involved in a colossal struggle with the Catholic Church. I'm not the first nut to think he might be a reincarnation of Sabbatai. Jacob Frank thought he was one, and he converted to Catholicism. He took a bunch of crazy other Jews with him, too. I don't know; it's almost like I've been placed in this position to make up for what he did. If the soul is the same, then it's always led other Jews to apostatize: with Frank to Catholicism, with Sevi to Islam. The only *Tiqqun* for such a soul is to draw lost or misplaced Jewish souls back into Judaism, to reverse the apostasy. If this be my purpose, then I'm ready to do what I can. But if it isn't, then all I need from you is a simple reassurance that I'm just suffering from an overactive imagination and I'll forget the whole thing. One thing I know. You're the key because you gave me the name that started my mind going. I guess I need a kind of physician for my soul. I don't have the kind of kabbalistic knowledge necessary to figure this one out on my own," Steve said.

"As I told you," the rabbi reiterated, "send me the details. I'll get back with you. God bless you, my son. Shalom."

Steve said good-by and hung up the phone. Then a chill came over him, and a tear to his eye. He was compelled to pick up a paper and pencil. A force of some kind seemed to be guiding his hand. He wroth Ruth's maiden name, *Harris*. Then he wrote it backwards . . . *Sirrah*. Hebrew is read backwards when compared to English. *Sirrah* and *Sarah* had the same letters in the same order in Hebrew. Steve had joked for years that he would have really believed the Sevi thing if only he had married a *Sarah*. Now he realized that he had.

There was a copy of the *Zohar* (the mystical Bible of Judaism) on his desk. He opened it and started to read. The portion seemed to call out to him. It taught that each soul has two halves, a male and a female. When both enter this world, they're only united if they live a life that's acceptable to God. If the two halves fail, they must wait to be reunited upon their return to heaven. Once any soul has learned its faults, it makes little sense to keep it out of this world, so it's sent back to try to improve over the last episode.

Steve liked the idea. He knew, as a science teacher, that reincarnation had never been proven, but then neither had the existence of God or even the human soul. The Zohar offered a romantic idea that captivated Ruth, too. What if he had been married to her in a previous life? The two, it could be argued, had loved each other so much that they had conquered death itself and a 10,000-mile separation at birth to return to be reunited. At a time when Ruth was beginning to feel the tension of the battle, the notion gave her a new and much needed outlook that would help her through the rough times. Steve never did become fully convinced that he was the gilgol of Sabbatai Sevi, but he knew a good thing when he saw it, and he loved to use the notion on his wife whenever she began to complain of the strain.

It was March 31, 1984, when Steve realized *Harris* = *Sirrah* backwards. That was the anniversary of the wedding of Sabbatai Sevi to Sarah, so he joked that the recognition was an "anniversary present" for his wife's soul.

Something else strange happened that night up in Philadelphia. Rabbi Shoulson had listened to Steve's tale of involvement with Islam. The rabbi had just converted a Catholic woman to Orthodox Judaism. That wasn't too unusual, although the convert (Mirium) first found it necessary to divorce her non-Jewish husband. What was strange about the case was that she was so enthralled with Mohammed that he thought she might have made a better Muslim convert than a Jewish one.

The rabbi decided to phone to ask whether or not she had ever heard of Steve's book or of its author.

When Mirium heard the rabbi ask if she knew of a Robinson, she nearly fell over. By some odd twist of fate, Mirium had worked for Steve's father when she lived in Fort Lauderdale. That was about two years earlier. Steve's father had given her a copy of the book, which had only sold a few hundred copies. Mirium was enthused about Mohammed for one reason only . . . Steve had sold her on the prophet to such a degree that she had become Robinson's most avid fan.

Mirium had written Steve so many letters that she had become somewhat of a nuisance to the author. One day after he had disavowed his own work, he called her and told her almost rudely that the best thing she could do was to run, not walk, to the nearest local rabbi, convert, and become a Jew. He thought that would "get her off his back." But while Steve wasn't being serious, Mirium actually moved to Trenton, New Jersey, drove to Philadelphia, met Shoulson and had him perform the conversion.

When Shoulson realized that the first person he asked about Robinson was one of the few in the world to be influenced by his book, and when he thought about the probability that his student should turn out to be the disciple of one he had circumcised 37 years before, he declared that this had to be "the finger of God." Still, he chose to not return Steve's letters for he neither welcomed the prospect of the return of Sabbatai Sevi, nor thought that Steve had yet proven God was with him in this life. One does not become a leading American rabbi by being too hasty. It was, he declared, better to wait and see what else would come to pass.

— 12 —
BENNET

Having received enough press to get a few million South Floridians buzzing about the case, and having filed in his pleadings all the evidence he had linking the Vatican to the Holocaust, Steve was now, ten days before the first scheduled hearing, ready to hire an attorney.

Bennet Cohen was the man to get the call. He was a somewhat short, slightly chunky 30-year-old who bore a remarkable resemblance to Dustin Hoffman.

The lawyer had seen the *Herald* article before Steve had called, and he was happy to take the case for he was aware of the value of publicity in building his own practice. What pleased him even more than getting the case, however, was the quality of most of the work that Steve had filed. No attorney could have, without dropping all other cases, carried out the amount of research that Steve had accomplished. The father had left no stone unturned in his efforts to be 100% thorough. His attack was blistering, and he had managed to expose a dozen or more outright errors by Schmidt or lies by his client. There was, Bennet told Steve, only one flaw with the father's efforts . . . the attack on the

Vatican and the amount of anti-Christian theology that was incorporated in Steve's pleadings.

"Christ!" exclaimed Bennet. "Where did you ever dig up this stuff on the Pope and the Nazis? It's dynamite, but are you nuts? The judge is Catholic! Schmidt will paint you as a fanatic and Watts will go right along with him. I'm gonna have to withdraw all this if I can."

"Oh, no you won't," Steve told his attorney. "You either take the case as is or not at all. We're not going to fight this war as 'apologists,' but as Jews seeking justice in an American court. I want to do more than just win custody. I'm trying to set the record straight on what the Vatican has done and on why it is that we Jews have refused to accept Jesus all these years. The true Messiah can never come until we have the courage to tell the world why we reject the false one."

"The articles you cite don't prove that the Vatican pulled the trigger; they just show that the Vatican kept its mouth shut when it knew all along what was happening."

"The Pope claims to be the spokesman for Christ and for God in this world. If a pope knew what was happening, and through his silence, allowed it to keep happening, it proves that he is no spokesman for God. A prime directive of any legitimate religion must be to teach mankind what is morally right and what is morally wrong. The leaders of the Roman Catholic Church have failed to accomplish this, and in so failing they have called into question the legitimacy of everything else they stand for."

Steve went on to offer Bennet five of the six million dollars he was asking for if the attorney would take the case against the Vatican on a contingency basis, but Bennet was more than a bit conservative about the effort and would only agree to handle the custody case itself for a hundred dollars an hour. He did promise to "consider" taking the Church suit, but was noncommittal about when he would actually help Steve file.

"Do you really want to start a holy war?" the attorney asked.

"If I have to, so be it. I'm not, however, asking you to kill anybody, just help me get the truth across in court," Steve told him. Robinson went on to explain the nature of the Biblical verses that were involved. Schmidt had taken the bait and included Steve's 24 scriptural references, which now meant (Steve hoped) that there would be an opportunity to actually debate the nature of Jesus during the trial.

"What do you want," Bennet again asked, "A second Sanhedrin to try Jesus? No judge is going to grant you that. The court is going to be concerned about one thing and one thing only . . . what's in the best interest of the child. You can't expect it to rule on which faith is right. Tell me about Bobby."

Steve told him of the years Bobby had spent in Hebrew and Sunday School, of the boy's service leadership, and about his excellence in all areas of Jewish studies.

Bennet cautioned him against trying to prep the boy for court, pointing out that judges burn parents for such behavior. Bobby should appear to act naturally on the stand. It was enough, Bennet thought, for the young man to simply identify with Judaism.

Steve spent about two hours with his new attorney during the initial session. He left with a good feeling and knew that it was best to have someone who was not emotionally involved serve as his spokesman before the judge.

Bennet's first call to the father was not one of good news. Schmidt was asking for a three-week continuance because he had not had time enough to digest the hundred-page Answer that Steve had filed. Bobby was by now suffering intensely from the struggle, and Steve had no desire to prolong his son's agony. He was, however, paying Bennet handsomely for his advice and the attorney thought it best not to vent their fury too early. "Judges," he said, "usually grant the first request for a continuance," so Steve agreed to go along with the delay.

About a week later Bennet informed his client that he had received an order from Watts for both parents to participate in mediation. Steve felt that because he had already tried to go that route the thing was really directed more at Carmen than him. He took the order as good news. Bennet advised him to "stay cool and be flexible." That wasn't too difficult, but he doubted that there was a chance in the world for Carmen to cooperate, too.

— 13 —
SURPRISE

If there was one virtue that Steve particularly lacked, it was patience. Monsignor Walsh had explained that it would be impossible to come up with a quick decision on the annulment, but as time wore on, the inertia of the custody case prohibited Steve's extending the time he could afford to wait before taking action. Still, he wanted the annulment more than any amount of money. The best recourse, he decided, was to have something in his hands that he could use in the interim for Court.

Robinson phoned the Archdiocese and informed it that he could put off the suit no longer unless the Monsignor would send him a simple letter stating that the baptism of Bobby was a serious mistake which would not have occurred if the priest had been aware of the circumstances. Walsh, anxious to head off the suit, complied with the demand instantly. The letter read as follows:

March 30, 1984

Dear Mr. Robinson:

Pursuant to your request, we are presently studying the validity of the baptism of your son Robert, which was performed on March 4, 1984.

In my opinion, had it been aware of the circumstances regarding your son's religious beliefs, the Church would not have performed the baptism on March 4, 1984.

Monsignor B. Walsh

When Steve received the letter, he was thrilled for he knew that it gave him much of what he needed. Now he had proof that the baptism had indeed occurred. It proved that the baptism was wrong in the eyes of a Monsignor, and it showed that Carmen had hidden the truth from the priest in her efforts to obtain the church sacrament. The document could, as Walsh had realized, be used by Steve in his custody battle. But it also provided the first piece of significant evidence for Robinson's planned suit of the Archdiocese itself. Walsh would probably later regret that he had been so hasty in granting Steve's request.

Armed with the just received admission, Steve drove off to Family Court where he would meet with Carmen for the ordered mediation. When he arrived (a half hour early), he was allowed to give the mediator, Mrs. Joanna Mills, a full run-down of his position before Carmen showed up. Carmen was unaware of his "advantage" when she walked into the office, but Steve didn't think it would really matter anyway for he was sure that his ex-wife would be as unbending as she had always been.

Carmen started out by stating that she was there against her will and then reminded Mills that mediation hadn't been successful before.

Joanna tried to emphasize the positive, pointing out that the two parents had been able to work together for three years without a problem.

Carmen told her that they could have gone on as before, but that Steve had poisoned her son's mind. Steve used Walsh's letter to embarrass his ex-wife, and the two traded accusations and denials for about ten minutes while Mills just sat there trying to get a better picture of the dynamics of the relationship.

It soon became apparent that Bobby was being hit for refusing to eat non-kosher food and for refusing to bow before statues of Jesus. Carmen saw the boy's refusal more in terms of disrespect for her and her family than as an honest expression of his true religious convictions.

"If you're so Christian, then why are you living out of wedlock with Ricardo Estavan?" Steve asked militantly.

"I don't live out of wedlock with anyone," Carmen said.

"What? Then where have I been picking up Bobby for the past month? Certainly not at your mother's anymore!" Steve asserted.

"I don't live out of wedlock with anyone!" Carmen repeated.

"Do you live at 534 Hummingbird Drive on Key Biscayne?" Steve asked.

"Yes, I do," Carmen answered.

"And is your phone number 427-9735?" he asked again.

"Yes, it is," his ex responded.

"Mrs. Mills. If you'll open a phone book and look up Ricardo Estavan, you'll see that he lives at that address and that's his phone number," Steve said as he reached for the phone directory.

"Ms. Rodriguez," Joanna asked, "if you live at that address and that's your phone number, then why not admit that what Mr. Robinson says is true?"

"Because . . . because . . . because we're married," Carmen said in a barely audible voice.

"What?" Steve asked as if in shock. "Can you prove that in a court of law?"

"Yes," Carmen said.

"Does Bobby know about this?" Steve wanted to know.

"No, we didn't tell him yet," Carmen revealed.

"Do you mean," Steve asked in total amazement, "that your son is living with you, and you get married, and you don't even tell him about it? What kind of mother are you? Mrs. Mills, this is why I want Bobby out of that house. There is no mother-son relationship here. My son is a hostage in a stranger's home!"

Mills had to agree. She turned to "Mrs. Estavan" and asked, "Why don't you try switching primary residency to the father? It sounds like the boy has a lot closer relationship with his dad than he does with you. Surely you want your son to be happy?"

Carmen took a hard look at Steve for the first time in the meeting. "What type of visitation would I have?" she asked.

Steve felt as if the heavens had just opened for him. The question implied that he just might have victory at hand. And yet it all seemed much too easy.

"What would you want?" he asked, realizing that this was the first time the two had ever been talking in terms of Carmen's visitation rather than his.

"Every Friday afternoon to Sunday afternoon," Carmen said innocently.

"You know that's impossible!" Steve exclaimed. "Bobby's in synagogue every Friday night. He'd miss it, but you'd be free to take him to church every Sunday."

"I want you to drive him up from Homestead, too," Carmen added.

Steve offered her every other weekend and told her he'd be willing to split the driving with her. It was about forty miles each way between the two homes, and he didn't want to get stuck with it all.

Carmen told him she'd consider it, and the meeting broke up with a promise that they'd discuss it more in another week. As the happy father drove away from court that day, he was singing at the top of his lungs. At last he thought, "my son is mine."

That afternoon was a visitation day for Steve. When Bobby got in the car, his father asked him, "Did your mother tell you anything about the mediation session today?"

"No, Daddy, what happened?"

"You mean that your mother didn't say anything about Ricardo?" Steve asked in disbelief.

"No, what happened? I want to know!" the boy said.

"I can't believe that your mother still didn't tell you. She married him! She's considering turning you over to me. I guess Ricardo doesn't want to pay a fortune to fight for someone else's kid!"

"That's fantastic! When will you know? Mom never tells me anything."

"In a week. We have to go back for another session. Your mother will bring you in before that time to talk to a Joanna Mills. Be careful about what you say around the house. Your mother may be upset if she learns I told you about the wedding," Steve warned him.

"O.K. I love you, Daddy. I can't wait to be with you all the time."

"I love you, too, son. Keep the faith. It looks like we're finally beginning to see the light at the end of the tunnel."

A few days later Carmen took her son to be interviewed by Mrs. Mills. Bobby, "feeling his oats," told the mediator that if given his say about visitation, he would limit it to an hour per week with his mother.

"But, Bobby," Joanna told him, "your mother loves you so much that she wants to make you happy by transferring primary residency to your father."

"If she loves me so much, why does she hit me almost every day?"

"I don't know, Bobby, probably from frustration because she thinks you don't love her."

"If you're serious, and I'm gonna live with Dad because she really wants to make me happy, and not because the judge is gonna order it, then I'll love her again and agree to see her more than an hour a week, uh, maybe one day a week."

"I'm sure that will make your mother happier," the

mediator said.

"Is she really gonna turn me over?" Bobby asked.

"I don't know. I hope so. Today she told me she's still thinking about it, but she isn't sure."

"God, I hope so," the boy said, "I get so many headaches from this fight and I can't sleep at night."

"Why do you want to live with your father so much?" the woman asked.

"Because we love each other so much. He always does fun things with me. At night we have pillow or slap fights before we go to sleep. I like those. Then he tells me stories. My dad's got a new story to tell every single night. He teaches me lots of neat stuff and never hits me if I do something wrong. He just talks to me about it and makes me understand. He's smart, too. I want to be just like him when I grow up. Besides, I'm Jewish and Mom hits me a lot when I won't kneel to Jesus or when I tell her I can't eat something because it's not kosher. I just want to live in peace, and Mom won't let me."

A few days later the parents were back again in the waiting room outside Joanna's office. Neither party would look at the other for the twenty minutes they waited, and the man could somehow feel that something had gone wrong. He worried that his big mouth might have done him in, that it was wrong to tell Bobby the details of the previous mediation session.

It soon became obvious that his fear was well founded. Bobby must have done something to give away his knowledge of the marriage, for upon appearing before Mills, Carmen announced that she had decided not to give in.

Steve's choice of language at that point was anything but

refined or religious. It took some time for the mediator to calm him down while Carmen just sat back and looked at the ceiling.

"You won't be satisfied until that kid totally hates your guts, will you?" Steve demanded. "Do you enjoy beating him? You do, don't you? I know how you think. Bobby is a miniature me, another Steve Robinson. In that sick head of yours, you really believe you're hitting me whenever you strike him, don't you? That shrink was right about you last time. You're nuts!"

"Why do you hit your son?" Joanna asked.

"I don't hit him that much," Carmen said, "but sometimes I have to because he shows no respect, not for me, my family, or my religion. I tell him, 'Bobby, if you don't respect Jesus, you don't love me.' He just looks up at the ceiling. I hate that, so I hit him . . . but not hard, just enough to get the point across."

"Mrs. Estavan, as a Christian, I must tell you that you can't beat the love of Christ into a child. I can't understand what meaning you might have thought baptism would have for someone who was as unaccepting of Jesus as your son is. Why did you want to baptize the boy knowing how he felt?" the mediator asked.

"Without baptism you've got to go to hell," Carmen said. "That's what I was taught as a child in a Catholic school."

Steve cut in and boasted, "If I have anything to do about it, your Church is gonna wind up teaching something very different before I'm through with it."

Carmen knew what he was up to. "I heard all about your threat. Mrs. Mills, this insane man is trying to sue the Vatican for six million dollars. That's why Monsignor Walsh wrote the letter he did," she declared. The woman was aware of Steve's plan because he had been goaded into answering questions about what he would do by a student in the hallway after class one day. The kid was a friend of Carmen's brother and word of the pending suit had gotten to her by the boy.

Mrs. Mills did her very best to arrange some type of agreement, but her efforts were in vain. Steve now suspected that Carmen's strategy had been to try to appear reasonable while really offering nothing. She had known all along that Steve would never have accepted primary residency without some way to take his son to synagogue. When the mediation confirmed that Bobby would still go every other week, she felt justified to fight on.

Robinson was troubled that his son would now have to endure so much more pain. And yet, in a way he also felt relief. Any quick agreement with Carmen was likely to include a promise not to sue the Vatican. Steve, however, wanted the annulment of the baptism every bit as much as he did primary residency. Without the annulment, Bobby's religious identity would always remain clouded.

To be sure, Steve would have taken the quick agreement had Carmen gone through with it. But, failing to achieve such a settlement, he rationalized that his "Karma" was not in the simple solution, but in the epic struggle that lay ahead with the new Roman Empire. David had to slay Goliath. When Carmen baptized Bobby without his consent, Steve had been given the "slingshot" needed to attack the giant. Walsh's letter provided the shot required to finish the job.

— 14 —
THE PRETRIAL CONFERENCE

The pretrial conference, a two-hour session before General Master Royce, was held in late April. Its purpose was to clarify the issues and list all potential parties to testify. No witnesses, however, were permitted to appear that day.

Schmidt was out of the country then so his assistant, Tom Branigan was left to carry the ball for Carmen. In Steve's corner were Steve himself, Bennet and another Jewish attorney, Steve Busker. Busker was an associate of Bennet, but he had tagged along purely out of interest in the case, and not for any compensation. Robinson, who was listed as a "co-counselor" on the case, was glad to have the extra help present.

Even before they could get into the meat of the session, Branigan opened up with a total lie. He claimed that Bennet had not delivered any pretrial catalog to Schmidt's office. (The pretrial catalog lists all major evidence and witnesses to be presented.) Bennet had in fact not only done so, but he had even carried it there personally. The two attorney's traded accusations for a while. Finally Cohen handed Branigan another copy of the catalog, and Branigan then apologized to the Court because his side had yet to prepare its own catalog.

Royce wanted to know exactly what each side was asking for. Bennet then realized that he needed to confer with his client. Steve wanted full custody, but under the new Uniform Joint Custody Act of Florida, that was nearly impossible to procure. You practically had to prove that the mother was a diseased prostitute with homicidal tendencies to completely remove a child from her care. "Carmen has problems," Steve told Bennet, "but nothing like that. By the court's standards, I guess I've got to settle for primary residency."

Carmen was also compelled to ask for nothing more than continued joint custody, though she, of course, sought to retain primary residency herself. Each side asked the other to pay for the legal costs of both. Both parties stated a willingness to give the other side "liberal visitation."

When Royce heard that both petitioners were prepared to settle for some form of joint custody, he asked each parent to admit that the other was "fit."

Carmen was willing to concede the point, but Steve wasn't.

"If I thought she was fit, Your Honor, I wouldn't have filed for custody," Robinson said.

"If you don't think she's fit, then you must ask for full custody," the general master responded. "But, I must warn you," he added, "that it would be very hard indeed for you to win it no matter what you say in court."

"Then," Steve said, "I'll admit that Mrs. Estavan is fit for visitation purposes in a joint-custody arrangement, but she isn't fit for primary residency."

Royce accepted the answer, and Carmen looked with disgust at her ex-husband. Steve glanced back at her and tried to remember what it had been like when he once loved her. That seemed like a million years ago. The person who sat across from him now was no more than a stranger and an enemy. He couldn't for all the world believe that he could have ever cared for her.

"Mr. Cohen, who will your witnesses be?" Royce asked.

"We will have a former president of Mr. Robinson's synagogue, the current vice president and the acting rabbi, all of whom are very familiar with both father and son. Mr. Robinson's boss, Dr. Clifford, will be present, as well as the mohel who circumcised Bobby seven years ago, witnesses to the circumcision, Bobby's Sunday school teacher, Archbishop McCarthy, and Bobby, himself," Bennet stated.

"We all know what Bobby's going to say," the general master declared. From the way the remark was made, it was apparent that he had either read the *Herald* article on Bobby, had spoken to Mrs. Mills, or both.

"And what will you attempt to prove at the trial?" Royce asked.

"We contend that the mother agreed to raise the child in question in the Jewish religion and that, to the detriment of the child who has developed a strong Jewish identity, the mother has gone back on that pledge by recently having Bobby baptized. Neither the child, nor the father who had joint custody, approved of the baptism, which was an act so outrageous as to merit a change in custody or, at a minimum, a change in primary residency. We will also prove that Mrs. Estavan is not herself a practicing Catholic,"

Bennet stated.

"How will you do that?" Royce asked.

"By showing that her new marriage was conducted not by a Catholic priest, but by a justice of the peace," Bennet answered.

The general master then questioned Branigan about Carmen's witnesses. None were listed save Carmen herself and her husband.

Branigan next proceeded to define the issues as his client saw them. "Mr. Robinson has systematically alienated the affections of the child from his mother," the attorney asserted, and then he added that, "He has secretly enrolled the boy in Hebrew school and used religion to drive a wedge between mother and son."

Royce wanted to know if any psychological evaluations had been done. Branigan was coy about the matter. He knew that Schmidt had sent Carmen to their own doctor, and he knew that the man's findings would support Mr. Robinson unless sufficient new motivation could be found to help change his mind, so for now he merely chose to keep the testing a secret.

Steve had strong feelings about the idea. "Your Honor," he said, "the last custody battle I fought with that lady involved expensive Court-ordered evaluations. They supported me, cost me a fortune, and I found that Judge Watts refused to abide by the recommendation given, namely that I be awarded custody. The psychologist recommended that my ex-wife should participate in psychotherapy if Bobby remained in her care, and Watts didn't order that either. Dr. Elinson predicted that we'd be back, and here we are. If his opinion were heeded the first time, none of us would have to go through the current ordeal. I haven't changed very much since the previous testing was done, nor has Mrs. Estavan. Bobby has matured a good bit, but as you apparently are aware, he still wants to live with me. I think more evaluations would only be a waste of money."

Royce asked Branigan how Carmen felt about the issue. After a brief conference, the attorney announced, "My client agrees to have the child evaluated only if Mr. Robinson will pay for it."

Bennet argued that the fee should be divided. He was concerned that the other side would have an easier time challenging results favoring Steve if it could claim the father had "bought" the report. Branigan refused to budge on the issue, knowing that it would make his doctor's report look better if he could argue that Carmen was just as entitled to pay for findings as Steve was. When Bennet heard the name of the psychologist, a Dr. Goldberg, he decided that it might not be such a bad idea to have an expert witness to call.

Branigan went on to complain about Steve's plan to subpoena the Archbishop, claiming such harassment was the reason that Carmen hadn't been married in the Church. Carmen's attorney also wanted time for pretrial depositions from all of Robinson's witnesses.

Royce checked his calendar, and found that, due to his upcoming vacation, there were no full-day openings for another two months. The trial was set for June 29, 1984. In the interim, Steve managed to get better visitation.

It was a Wednesday afternoon, so the father drove over to pick up his son when the hearing broke up. Bobby was full of hope of a quick resolution to his problem. Steve hated to let his son down, so he took the boy to the planetarium to help get his mind off the new wait. Bobby cuddled up to his dad in the car and reassured him that he was willing to hold out for the duration. "I know," the boy said, "that one day when you come to pick me up, it will be for good."

Bobby told his dad about Carmen's psychologist, Dr. Gray, in the car that day, but when Steve later called, the doctor refused to speak with him.

— 15 —
THE NEW "EXPERTS"

Dr. Goldberg proved to be Jewish as Bennet had expected from the name. He spent about three hours interviewing and testing Bobby and was awed by the devotion the boy showed for his father. The doctor also interviewed both parents and spoke at length with Steve over the phone on seven occasions.

Goldberg, a former associate of Dr. Elinson, agreed that Steve was the primary psychological parent, but he was concerned by the degree of surface hatred that Bobby displayed towards his mother, an emotion not confirmed by all of the projective testing methods he applied.

When asked to draw a picture of his mom, Bobby drew a witch with the word "bad" on her chest. Then he erased the word and drew a bat in its place. Yet in story-telling tests, there were no harsh feelings that came forth. The meaning of all this was clear to Goldberg. Bobby "knew" that he was supposed to hate his mother, but that feeling was not apparent at the subconscious level.

The child had only praise for his father, but the praise was seen as being extreme. Goldberg sympathized with

Steve as a fellow Jew, but he felt that Bobby was too involved with religion for a seven-year-old. Although tests confirmed that the boy had an I.Q. in excess of 150, the doctor still couldn't believe that the child really understood all the Bible verses taught to him by his father. What concerned him most, however, was that Bobby was having a hard time getting acceptable food while he was over at his mother's home.

The doctor was also afraid to come down too strongly on Steve's side for he knew that such results would be tainted by the fact that he was a Jew, too. It was best, he thought, to appear to be impartial, no matter how many stories of beatings and food deprivation. Bobby looked healthy enough and there were no marks to indicate serious abuse.

The months in between court sessions also featured a visit by another H.R.S. social worker, James O'Malley. With a name like that, Steve suspected at once, and correctly, that the Catholic viewpoint would eventually be represented.

The night before O'Malley arrived was a busy one at the Robinson home. The family wallpapered Bobby's bedroom and an adjoining bathroom to make the house look like a proper place to raise a kid. From the way Bobby's room was set up with rocket and jet models dangling from the ceiling, and a well-arranged collection of new toys and books, you'd think that Steve was a stage prop designer by trade. Everything was finished a mere five minutes before O'Malley's arrival.

When the social worker began the interview, Bobby was not permitted to be in the room with the adults. O'Malley indicated that he had read the file, including the *Miami Herald* story and the evidence in the pleadings which linked the Vatican to the Holocaust. He didn't discuss these things much with Steve however, preferring to see what opinion, if any, the boy had of them.

Steve liked much of what he initially heard that day. For one thing, Carmen had so far refused to see the man, and O'Malley was quick to point out such continued behavior would hurt her case a lot.

The old man sat back and fired questions at the Robinson's for about an hour, taking notes and smiling kindly all the while. When he had listed all Steve's concerns, he called Bobby out of the bedroom and told the child that they were now going to have their "man-to-man secret talk," a discussion that Bobby had to promise not to share with his dad.

The secret interview was conducted in Bobby's room. O'Malley was quick to note that half the toys in the room had Israeli decals on them. It looked like the boy was preparing for a private war with the Arabs. There were Israeli jets, tanks, Uzi machine guns and half-tracks, not to mention a number of Jewish flags. "This," James thought, "is how the father brainwashes his son."

The discussion soon turned into O'Malley's private "crusade." He disliked Jews and this kid was a super Jew. For over an hour the seven-year-old spewed verse after verse to debate the man, trying to show why major beliefs of Christianity were in error. Carmen's old fears of Steve telling Bobby about the Holocaust were proven well-founded. The kid knew about each and every article that had been cited as evidence in the case, and O'Malley was hard pressed to refute any of it. Little questioning was needed about how the boy saw each of his parents. The social worker noted that in Bobby's eyes, the father could do no wrong and the mother could do no right.

"Why don't you love your mother?" he asked.

"Because she always hits me and gives me food I can't eat like ham which isn't kosher."

"What's wrong with ham? I eat it all the time," O'Malley exclaimed.

"The Torah says we can't eat it. Some laws are easy to understand, like the one that says not to murder. Others we don't understand, but we do them because God asked us to. Kosher laws are like that. We do them just to prove we love God enough to listen to Him. My dad says that God loves us more when we give up something we like just to please Him."

"Doesn't the Torah say anything about honoring your father and your *Mother* ?" the social worker asked.

Bobby didn't want to answer that one, so he changed the topic. "I've got a constitutionally guaranteed right to freedom of religion," the kid said.

"Seems to me every mother has a God-given right to expect obedience from her son, too," O'Malley said.

When the interview was over, O'Malley felt like he had just been through a war. In twenty-five years of interviewing kids, he had never encountered a child anywhere near Bobby's age who could quote the Constitution or the Scriptures like this child did. The boy was sure about what he believed, but O'Malley was just as sure that he really wanted to smack the little fellow. Still, his report would have to wait for Carmen to soften up to let him in. Perhaps, he thought, he might gain access to the mother by telling her over the phone about the "brainwashing" he had seen.

When O'Malley emerged from Bobby's room, he looked with exhaustion at Steve and said, "Well, Mr. Robinson, I have the picture here. I'm sure that the boy's mother will eventually see me. Please don't call my office after the report is written. I won't be able to discuss it."

By the time O'Malley left, Steve wasn't feeling too confident. Concerned about the strength of his case, he decided to call Monsignor Walsh's office to turn up the heat on the Church.

Walsh was about to leave for a trip to the Far East where he would meet the Pope. He wouldn't reveal whether or not Bobby would be discussed, but Steve gathered from the man's tone that such a dialogue was probable. Still, the Monsignor was elusive. Robinson thought it wise to remind the man that he couldn't wait forever before filing the suit against the Church.

"The court is not likely to rule in your favor. For it to do so would be a violation of the separation of Church and State," Walsh asserted.

Steve reminded him that, as an author, he could only benefit by national publicity, even if he lost his case. The Church, on the other hand, could only lose by having the Holocaust material exposed to the public. "If I win, I get the money," Steve said, "but if I lose, I'll still sell a million books. All I'm asking for is a simple letter stating that Bobby's baptism has been annulled. Your decision should be an easy matter."

If Walsh had been uncertain about discussing the subject with the Pope before, he now knew that there was no way out. This was a decision that couldn't be made at the local level. The very essence of baptism's meaning was at stake.

"Have a nice trip," Steve said as the conversation broke off. He knew that he had argued persuasively . . . but would the decision come in time? June 29th was now a mere three weeks away.

A week passed. When Steve checked his teacher mailbox, he found a message from Bennet. Apparently, Dr. Goldberg had finished his report and recommendations. Three times he tried to reach the attorney, but Bennet was in court each time. At last he got through and was given the answer.

"He recommends you be given primary residency for a trial period of one summer. Goldberg says that Bobby identifies with you and with the Jewish faith, but the boy's afraid of losing his mother in the battle. The doctor also recommends counseling," Bennet said.

"Is this guy serious, just a summer? I've been getting Bobby for most of the past two summers! That won't prove anything. We'll just be back in court again in another two months!" Steve exclaimed.

"Talk to the doctor," Bennet advised. "Maybe you can convince him to extend the trial period. I've got to tell you, however, that he won't be the only psychologist testifying. Carmen hired another so-called expert, a Dr. Gray. I've just received notice of his appearance from Schmidt."

"Terrific," Steve said sarcastically, "I know about the S.O.B. and I've tried to call him. He won't talk to me. Can't we block his testimony? He's not court-appointed and he hasn't even heard my viewpoint."

Bennet promised to do the best he could.

The following day Steve received a call from Mike Fitzpatrick, attorney for the Archdiocese of Miami. Mike said that the letter Steve wanted had been prepared and would soon be ready for release. Robinson was overjoyed. Without even thinking, he told the Church attorney that he needed the letter before the court hearing now only 13 days away. Fitzpatrick told him that the Archbishop would still need to sign it, but that shouldn't take too long. All he needed to know was where to send it when complete.

As soon as the attorney hung up after getting Steve's address, he realized that the Church might be letting itself in for more trouble by releasing the document before Bobby's custody trial. His biggest concern was that it would devastate the mother's case so thoroughly as to set up the Archdiocese for a suit by her. She might well make a case that the Church's actions had cost her a son. They'd be right back again looking at another large court action. Thus he thought it best to call McCarthy and advise not that the letter be destroyed, but "put on ice."

McCarthy concurred. He had given the matter much consideration and felt that the document should only be released at the last possible moment. Judge Watts, after all, was a practicing Catholic. It was unlikely that Steve or his attorney would be foolish enough to litigate against the Church until after the general master had ruled and Watts had had the opportunity to review the case. That could be months from then. By the next day Bennet had been informed that there would be a "delay while the letter worked its way through Church hierarchy."

— 16 —
THE DEPOSITIONS

Schmidt made certain to depose all of Robinson's witnesses before turning his attention to the main foe. None of them had yielded anything that could be used against the father so it was now time to do battle with the man who thought he knew so much.

Steve showed up at his enemy's office without Bennet to advise him. He was familiar with the process from the past bout with Carmen and was anxious to keep his legal costs as low as possible. Besides, he thought, he didn't want an attorney to stifle his responses. Bennet was always so cautious, something that Steve was bothered by when it came to defending the faith.

The questions were easy at first . . . name, address, occupation, etc. Then the attorney began to delve into *The Great Christ Debate*.

"You say in here that Jesus was the Messiah, isn't that correct?" Schmidt asked.

"In a matter of speaking, I did, but not in the Christian sense of the term. I supported the Moslem concept then, that Jesus was one of a continuing series of prophets." Steve said.

"Do you still hold that belief?" Schmidt wanted to know.

"No. I maintain a very high degree of respect for the Koran and for my Muslim cousins. But I now totally reject Jesus. I think he was a false prophet," Steve answered.

"Isn't that highly inconsistent of you? What made you change your mind?" Schmidt asked.

"Your client and her mother did a very good job of doing that. The two convinced me that when Jesus said in Luke 14:26, 'if any man come to me, and *hate* not his father, and mother, and wife, and children, and brothers, and sisters . . . and his own life also, he cannot be my disciple,' he meant it. I made excuses for his promise of division when I wrote the book, but I'm not wed to a Christian now and I needn't rationalize 'Christ's' remarks anymore. Yes, I once preached in his favor in synagogues. But the closer I drew to him, the more I found that my Christian in-laws hated me. I've developed such a bad taste in my mouth for the man now that I see him more as an anti-Christ than as a Christ."

"What do you mean by anti-Christ?" the attorney asked.

"The prime role of the Jewish Messiah is to bring peace — not in heaven but here amongst the nations. Jesus said, 'think not that I've come to bring peace on earth, I've come not for peace, but for division or the sword.' The prefix *Anti* means against. *Christ* is Greek for the Hebrew *Meshiach* or *Messiah*. As Jesus has claimed for himself a role against or opposite that of Isaiah's predicted 'Prince of Peace,' it can only be said that he has laid claim to the role

Anti-Messiah or *Anti-Christ*. That, in a nutshell, is my current view of the man."

"How do you explain all the people who saw the resurrected Christ?" Schmidt asked.

"There's an important common thread that runs through the Gospels," Robinson said. "It's one I missed in my original research . . . failure of those who knew Jesus to clearly recognize him after the Cross. In Matthew 28:17 we read of their doubt. In Mark 16:12 we're told that Jesus appeared *in another form*. In the 24th chapter of Luke we find that although the apostles were told by Jesus of a return on the third day, which it then was, and although they had been told by Mary Magdalene that she had seen the risen Christ, still when they themselves met him, 'their eyes were kept from recognizing him' for what must have been around six hours or so. In John's story, Mary Magdalene at first thought the risen Jesus to be 'the gardener.' And as for the tale of Doubting Thomas, it's missing from the snyoptic Gospels. It took sixty years for someone to fabricate the story and for it to make its way into John's account. I now believe that someone who didn't even look like Jesus succeeded in impersonating the slain rabbi."

"Why would anyone want to do that?" Schmidt asked.

"I can't say. Perhaps the impostor thought he would be proclaimed 'King of the Jews.' Maybe he was just playing a sick joke on those who refused to believe that Jesus was gone. Or he might have been following Jesus' instructions. We can only speculate what happened. There's one other possible explanation besides that of an impostor."

"Which is?" Schmidt asked.

"Well, I must say," Steve answered, "having been in the

tomb of Jesus, that while much has been made of a stone that had blocked the front of it while he was there, nothing is said in the New Testament about the fact that there is a window in the tomb leading out the back way. Jesus was only on the cross for about nine hours. It usually took two days to die up there. If he survived the cross and piercing (though unconscious at first) and was placed in the tomb still alive, he could have slipped out or been taken out by way of that window. Later when he was well enough to walk about, he might have disguised himself to keep from being caught and thrown back on the cross again. Thus the stories about his friends not recognizing him until they heard his voice. Who knows?"

Schmidt then asked about events preceding Bobby's delivery.

"I have here a copy of the records from Cedars of Lebanon Hospital concerning the birth of your son. You list his religion as Monotheistic, not Jewish. Why?"

"When I wrote the book," Steve answered, "I anticipated starting a new faith for those like my son who were not fortunate enough to have been born Jewish. The gentiles needed a religion that taught the proper view of the Almighty. Monotheism means the belief in One God. The faith I envisioned starting would've been modeled after basic Jewish theology. It would have opposed both the Trinity and the doctrine of vicarious atonement, concentrating instead on the concept of individual responsibility, and on morality based upon the "Seven Precepts of Noah" (maintain courts of justice; commit no murder, theft, incest or adultry, blasphemy, idol worship, or cruelty to animals). But after Bobby was born, Carmen and I decided to include

Bobby in the Jewish covenant, thus the brith milah. With the passage of time, I came to view an expanded Judaism, that is, a proselytizing variety of it as a more fulfilling alternative for gentiles. So I dropped the idea of "Monotheism" and returned to a more traditional Jewish belief. I also came to understand that theological compromise can never guarantee family harmony."

Schmidt decided to go for the jugular vein. "Does the name Sabbatai mean anything to you?" he asked.

Steve knew right away that one of his students had leaked the story to Carmen. The teacher had used the coincidental links between himself and the Turk during a lecture on the differences between science and superstition. His kids had been given most of the facts and then were asked to use scientific logic to pick the story apart. Steve loved to do things like that during the first week of every science course he ever taught. If the students failed to destroy the implications of his story, he would show them how the scientific approach would. Yet he knew that Schmidt would only bring up the topic in an attempt to prove him to be mad, so he resolved to give the attorney no more information that was absolutely necessary.

"Yes," Robinson admitted, "the name does mean something. It's part of my Hebrew name."

"Does it have any particular religious significance?" Schmidt asked.

"The name's a common one, often given to someone who's born on the Sabbath," Steve said.

"Did you ever tell anyone that you're a reincarnation of a man who had his head cut off?" Schmidt inquired.

Steve didn't want to lie under oath, but he quickly

realized that the question had been improperly phrased anyway. Sevi had *NOT* had his cut; he was only threatened with beheading.

"No," Steve said smugly, "I know nothing of any man who was beheaded."

"Did you ever tell anyone that you got the scar on your neck because you were beheaded in a previous life?" Schmidt asked again.

Steve laughed and said, "I got the scar on my neck when a cyst the size of a grapefruit was cut out of my neck in *THIS* life! Your question is absurd!"

"I have no further questions. You'll be able to see the transcripts of the deposition in about five days if we use them. You have the right to make any corrections you like at that time. Thank you," the attorney said. With that, the meeting was over. Schmidt never did have the interview transcribed.

Robinson remained concerned about the Sevi questions. He soon learned that the "Judas" student was Rico Gonzales, a boy thrown out of his class for misconduct. This meant that it would be necessary to cue Bennet in on Sabbatai Sevi and to ask the attorney to subpoena the lad's grades and disciplinary record. That way any "tales of reincarnation" would be tainted by Rico's history of persistent misconduct and suspensions.

When the teacher phoned his attorney, he discovered that Bennet hadn't yet subpoenaed the mohel, Cantor Lipson. Steve was furious. Bennet urged him to calm down while he phoned the Cantor. Then the lawyer had to break the news to his client that Lipson was only four hours away from flying off to Europe on a summer vacation.

"Get over to his home or out to the airport now and preserve his testimony in a deposition!" Steve demanded.

Bennet did his best to set the thing up. He was lucky to get a court reporter, but he couldn't reach Schmidt to inform him of the deposition. Within two hours the crucial story was ready to be transcribed, but Bennet knew that without Schmidt there to cross-examine the witness, Lipson's statements would probably be inadmissible even though Steve had paid hundreds to preserve them.

Having waited too long to guarantee Lipson's testimony, Bennet finally subpoenaed Carmen to bring Bobby to court. That turned out to be no easy feat. Carmen refused to open the door, and before it was all over, there was such a disturbance outside her home that she called the police to "remove the trespassers." The cops came all right, but they helped nail her with the order. Bobby, it seemed, would finally have his day in court.

— 17 —
THE STIPULATION

When trial day finally rolled around, there was a small army of friends and family members who showed up ready to back Steve. It seemed like half the Homestead Jewish Center congregation was there to make sure that nobody would keep their little Bobby from them any longer.

This time Steve was on good terms with his parents who were present while Carmen's were not. He took their absence as a sign of repentance for past deeds. In Carmen's corner were two strangers. One turned out to be her new husband. The other was Dr. Gray. Schmidt was there (without Branigan) and "Judas" Gonzales was present, too, (lacking the guts to look directly at his former teacher). Steve was glad they were ready for the kid.

One important witness was *not* present . . . Bobby. Carmen had decided to defy the subpoena. She had left the boy home with a baby-sitter. Also missing were O'Malley's recommendations. Carmen had only let him in for an interview three days before the trial, not enough time for the social worker to get the report done. Nor had Bennet been able to make any progress with the Archdiocese attorneys.

Steve was so angry about the Church stonewalling that he insisted Bennet file the six-million-dollar suit posthaste. Bennet, however, remained cool to the idea. "There's plenty of time for that," he calmly said, "Wait till after we get a ruling here, and the Judge has a chance to sign the order, assuming it favors us."

When it became obvious that Carmen wouldn't deliver Bobby, Bennet's associate, Steve Busker, phoned the process server.

While Busker was gone, Royce summoned the principle parties with a warning that he could only devote two and a half hours to the case that day, far less than the attorneys had planned for. Robinson was furious but tried not to show it. There was no way he would be able to get even half his witnesses in. "This is what I had to wait five months for?" he asked Bennet.

"We'll start with Dr. Goldberg as planned. I hope you managed to sway him about the extended trial residency," the attorney said.

After the preliminaries were over, Cohen was allowed to address the Court first.

"Your Honor, if I may start by addressing a problem we had in preparing for trial. One of our key witnesses, the mohel, Cantor Lipson, is out of the country in Europe on vacation. I only found out about his intentions to depart on the day of his trip. At that time I phoned Mr. Schmidt's office to notify him of a deposition that I took the same day. Mr. Schmidt was unavailable, being at sea on his boat. Please note that my opponent has also listed Cantor Lipson as a witness on his pretrial catalog. We have preserved the Cantor's testimony which is highly critical to our case, and we ask that you admit into evidence said deposition now."

Schmidt then rose to squelch the request. "Your Honor," he said, "it is critical that we be given the opportunity to cross-examine the Cantor. It's impossible to cross-examine a deposition. Mr. Cohen had sufficient time to notify his witness of the trial, and he failed to do so until it was too late. I can't be expected to be sitting around waiting for him to catch up on important details."

"Seems to me that Mr. Schmidt is entitled to enjoy his boat from time to time. Your request to include the deposition is denied, Mr. Cohen," the general master said.

"I understand, Your Honor, but I'd like to include the deposition in the court file on an unofficial basis." Bennet then handed the document over to Royce who accepted it.

"The second item I would like to address concerns a subpoena that I had delivered to Mrs. Estavan. The order called for her to deliver the child here today. Bobby was lawfully served with his mother in the presence of two Key Biscayne police officers who included said serving in a police report that they filed. We haven't seen the child here today, and we wish to ask Mr. Schmidt if his client is not now in contempt of court."

"Your Honor, this is a vicious lie. I can state categorically that my client was never served with a subpoena for Bobby."

Bennet was astounded by Schmidt's perversion of the truth. Apparently his opponent chose to take advantage of the fact that the trial would probably be too short to have his position successfully challenged. "Your Honor," Cohen said, "I'm surprised to see Mr. Schmidt mislead the court about something so easy to prove. My associate is now attempting to reach the process server. He should have him here within a half hour."

"I have no objections to your attempts to bring in the server, but I must inform you that I won't promise to put a seven-year-old on the stand to testify against his mother. Call in your first witness," Royce said.

Dr. Goldberg was sworn in and the questioning began. The doctor first stated his credentials, then discussed the tests he administered, and finally summed up the history of the dispute.

"Mr. Robinson," Goldberg said, "is a quite active Conservative Jew. He claims that his ex-wife promised to raise Bobby as a Jew at the boy's Brith Milah, or ritual circumcision. Mrs. Estavan, on the other hand, has recently become active in the Catholic religion, and she endeavored to convert Bobby to her faith by baptizing him and enrolling him in catechism class, an activity that she has removed him from recently. Both parents are subjecting the child to great pressures to adopt their respective faiths."

"Does the child have any particular religious preference of his own?" Bennet asked.

"Bobby is just seven, and while I question the depth of his theological understanding, I must say that he does identify very strongly with the Jewish faith," Goldberg said.

"What is the evidence for the strength of his identification with Judaism?" the attorney asked.

"Bobby refuses to eat non-kosher food in his mother's home. It was apparent both through his testimony and his mother's that he'd rather be beaten than forced into violating the kosher dietary laws. From what I've been able to determine in speaking with his catechism teacher, Bobby was highly verbal in class there about both his Jewish beliefs and his rejection of Jesus. The instructor informed me that she and her church advised Mrs. Estavan it was in the child's best interests that he be withdrawn from her class. Mrs. Estavan complied with that advice."

"Do you think that it's healthy for Bobby to be exposed to both religions?" Cohen asked.

"Under normal or average circumstances, I'd see no problem with such a solution. But this child is so strongly identified with Jewish beliefs as to render a Catholic exposure harmful to his well being," the doctor said.

Bennet then pointed out that, in accordance with Carmen's answers to his interrogatories, it was the mother's intention to send her son to a full-time Catholic parochial school if she won the case. Goldberg saw her plan as disastrous, pointing out that a boy so vocally against Christ would constantly invite personal physical assault in such a situation.

There was some discussion about Bobby's high I.Q., but Bennet couldn't quite succeed in leading the doctor to conclude that Bobby really understood all the theology he pretended to know.

The pictures of Carmen drawn by her son were more powerful than any direct quotations that were read to the Court. The psychologist testified that Bobby saw his mother in a very negative way. Dr. Goldberg seemed to place more emphasis on the pictures than on the other projective testing methods which had given him such concern in his earlier report. He now realized Bobby did have the intelligence to know that while he had a problem with his own mother, not all women were like her. It was less than fair to judge his attitude toward Carmen on the basis of the boy's refusal to generalize about all women.

"Based on your observations," Bennet asked, "were you able to reach any conclusion about placing Bobby with one of his parents?"

"I was. I believe that on a temporary basis, primary residency should be with the father for a trial period of six months, and that all parties concerned should be required to undergo family counseling for the duration of the recommended order."

Bennet then turned the witness over to Schmidt.

"Dr. Goldberg," the lawyer bellowed, "in your original report you said that you would recommend a custody or residency switch of just a summer. Have you changed your mind, and if so, why?"

"I have altered my opinion. Mr. Robinson convinced me that a summer trial period was too short, being equal to what he was accustomed to having over the past few years. Too short a trial exchange would not encourage the mother to participate in therapy or counseling in any kind of a meaningful way."

"I noticed," Schmidt said, "that you have a copy of Dr. Elinson's first evaluation in your file. How did you come to possess it?"

"Mr. Robinson gave it to me," the doctor admitted. He then went on to state that he had been Elinson's former associate.

"How much did Dr. Elinson's four-year-old report influence your decision?" Schmidt asked.

"Very little. I formed my opinion largely on the basis of my own research; however, it should be stated that I asked both parties to produce any data that they thought might be relevant. Mr. Robinson also supplied me with the social worker's report from the past custody battle."

Schmidt wanted to know what both reports recommended. The doctor stated that the two were in agreement about placement of the child with his father.

"Let the record indicate," Schmidt argued, "that Dr. Goldberg did not form his opinion until he had first reviewed these prejudicial reports. Tell me, Doctor, who took Bobby to your office?"

"On both occasions it was the father who brought him in," Goldberg answered.

"Don't you think that Mr. Robinson could have filled the boy's head with all sorts of thoughts against his mother just before you saw him?" the lawyer asked.

"It's possible, though I saw no evidence of any prep work being done."

"Could Mr. Robinson hear or see his son while you were interviewing him?" Schmidt asked.

The psychologist assured the Court that the testing occurred in an isolated setting and that the father's presence in the waiting room was not a factor. He pointed out that Dr. Elinson had obtained similar results four years before and that it was the mother who had then brought the boy in.

Goldberg's testimony went on for nearly two hours. By the time he had finished, Busker had been successful in summoning the process server. Cohen informed the general master, but Royce was more interested in emptying his bladder than in hearing about Carmen's contempt of court. He declared a five-minute recess and promised to rule on the next witness when he got back.

Bennet was pleased by the psychologist's testimony, but was almost as disturbed as Steve was about the time left, now a mere thirty minutes.

After the break, Royce announced that he couldn't afford to waste time by seeing the process server. Instead, he wanted to hear from Schmidt's prime witness, who turned out to be Dr. Gray.

The "hired gun" was so highly effeminate that Busker soon found himself unable to control his laughter. "Is his name Dr. Gray or Dr. Gay?" the father also chuckled just loud enough to be heard by all.

Gray puckered up his lips and then gave a dirty look to Robinson, who he hadn't previously seen. He then began to recite his credentials which included experience testifying (for a fee) in over 500 custody cases throughout his career. The doctor had spent four hours testing Bobby and several hours listening to Carmen's side of the story.

"Why did Mrs. Estavan approach you?" Schmidt asked.

"The Mrs. related to me a great concern over how it was that Mr. Robinson was poisoning the boy's mind against her. She said that the father was teaching him to hate her, her family and Jesus."

"Did you discuss religion or question Bobby about it at all?" the attorney asked.

"No, why should I? The boy's too young to be burdened with such matters," the doctor stated while noticeably batting his eyelashes. By now Bennet was starting to giggle, and it was easy to see that his opponent was plainly embarrassed by the demeanor of the witness. There was a smile coming over Royce's face as well. As Schmidt pushed on, Bennet and his client began to pay as much attention to the general master's reaction as to the psychologist's responses.

"Dr. Goldberg claims that Bobby saw his mother as the embodiment of evil while seeing his father as the essence of good. Do your findings agree with his?"

Gray licked the top of his lip with his tongue in a nearly obscene fashion, and Cohen nearly fell onto the floor. Busker was in stitches, too, and the general master had to caution him to control himself lest he be thrown out of the hearing.

"No," the doctor proclaimed, "not at all. I found that Bobby loves both parents equally, though he does identify with Daddy a bit more than with Mommy at this age, something totally within the norm for a six-year-old *male*." The man seemed to stress the last word with a certain sexual relish.

"Do you have any pictures that Bobby drew of his father or mother?" Schmidt inquired.

"Not with me, but they were *all* very nice drawings. As I said, he loves both parents."

"Mr. Robinson and Dr. Goldberg are both opposed to exposing Bobby to Catholicism as well as Judaism. Do you anticipate any problems from such a dual exposure?" Schmidt asked.

"I think both parents should downplay the religion. Let the boy choose. But I don't see anything wrong or harmful about exposing the boy to our Lord. I think that Mr. Robinson has been behaving totally unreasonably. The child has a Catholic mother. Why shouldn't she have as much right as he does to teach about how to worship God?" Gray answered.

"Based on your evaluations, were you able to reach a recommendation concerning custody?" Schmidt wanted to know.

Gray was angry because of Steve's apparent derision of him. The doctor's report initially blasted Robinson, but made no final recommendation. Now that he had seen the father, he felt compelled to do him in.

"I see no strong reasons to switch custody at this time. I do think that the parents should participate in family therapy of some kind," Gray said.

"Thank you. Your witness, Mr. Cohen," Schmidt said with relief.

"I notice," Bennet began, "that you have a copy of the *Miami Herald* clipping about this fight in your file. Who gave it to you?"

"My secretary."

"You said that you interviewed the child and his mother. What about the father?" Bennet asked.

"No, I didn't speak to him. Why should I?"

"Did Mr. Robinson ever call your office to try to reach you?" Bennet inquired.

"Yes," Gray admitted. "But I didn't have time to talk to him. I'm a busy man."

"When did Mrs. Estavan bring Bobby in to see you?" Bennet asked.

"Around the end of March or the beginning of April. I can't remember when," Gray said.

At this point Royce declared that Dr. Gray had more than enough time to speak with Bobby's father. It was obvious the general master lent no credence to anything the psychologist had to say from then on.

"Did Bobby tell you about his mother hitting him?" Bennet asked.

Gray admitted a number of beating incidents related by the boy, all of which he chose to leave out of his report. "His mother hits him," the doctor said, "because he's a very naughty boy. He won't eat the food in her house."

"Do you know what the word *Kosher* means?" Bennet inquired.

"No," Gray said, "I have no idea."

"Do you know anything about the Jewish religion?" Bennet asked again.

"No, I don't know what Jews believe in and I don't care either."

By now Royce was becoming angry. "I don't believe you didn't know the boy was being hit for religious reasons. If you knew he wasn't happy with the food in his mother's home, you had a responsibility to point that out in your report. Why didn't you?" the general master asked.

"I didn't think it was important. Lots of kids don't like the food they're offered. Look at how many youngsters don't like spinach or liver!"

Steve asked Bennet to get rid of Gray then, but his lawyer was certain that the longer the psychologist testified, the more he would harm Schmidt's case.

Bennet managed to get Gray to admit that he had formed his sole opinion of Robinson through the *Miami Herald* article in which Bobby had called Jesus a false prophet. As Bennet's questions grew more and more hostile, Gray's support of Carmen became ever stronger.

"Religious differences are no reason to switch custody," the doctor asserted."

"Even when a child is religiously opposed to eating the food that his mother is forcing on him in contradiction to the child's faith?" Royce asked.

"That's right. Ham or bacon won't hurt the boy. If he wants to be a Jew when he grows up, he can always be one then. In the meantime, he needs to learn respect for his mother. I don't think religion is ever worth fighting about," Gray said.

"You know," Royce stated, "even Saint Paul said *No food is unclean unless the one who eats it thinks it is, and then it is unclean for that person.* As for religion not being worth fighting about, unfortunately when we look around the world, that doesn't seem to be the general consensus of humanity. Men have always gone to war over religious differences, and these parents are at it again here with this little boy serving as the battlefield for the latest clash in a two-thousand-year-old feud. I don't believe religious differences can be anymore overlooked here today than they can be in the Middle East or Ireland. You're dismissed, Mr. Gray. I believe I've heard enough and read enough to get the picture. Gentlemen, if your clients are willing to stipulate to a decision based upon the testimony of the two psychologists who have appeared today, I'll give you a judgment in about ten days. We'll take another five-minute break now. If you want to continue the trial, it won't be until September at the earliest that I can hear more testimony."

In the waiting room Robinson broke the news to all his supporters. It looked promising, but Steve didn't like the idea of waiting ten days.

"Be patient," Bennet advised. "These guys don't like to look a mother in the face when they rip a child from her.

Besides, he's probably got to decide on what visitation to order. We've given him a mountain of paperwork to digest, too. The man needs time. Have faith. From everything I saw in there, we've got him in our pocket."

"We're waiving a lot more witnesses than they are. All they have left is the Sabbatai Sevi thing, and we're ready for it. You're the lawyer, Bennet. If you think we've won, I'll gamble you're right," Robinson said as they returned to the hearing.

Both parties agreed to the master's stipulation. Royce wanted to know what visitation each would agree to give the other and both parents tried to seem generous. It was a futile exercise, however, for the master knew what he would have to order anyway.

Steve went on summer active duty with the Coast Guard the next day. He tried to concentrate on his new job, but it wasn't easy as each day seemed like an eternity until the verdict was in.

— 18 —
THE DECISION

Two and a half weeks passed. On a Friday afternoon Steve found a note in his teacher's mailbox requesting a call to his attorney.

"Let's see," Bennet said, "It just came in . . . the good stuff starts in paragraph 2. Quote. The report of Dr. Goldberg discloses that the child is experiencing an excessive amount of emotional conflict concerned both with pleasing both parents and fearing that he may permanently lose one or the other at the conclusion of this fight. That Bobby identifies himself as a Jew. It further appears that the husband had fervently embraced Conservative Judaism in which he had deeply involved his son; to the extent that the child had adopted the dietary laws of that faith and refused to eat in the mother's home until the mother began trying to provide for his dietary needs."

"What else?" Steve asked.

"It rambles on about the baptism . . . the expert witnesses disagreed . . . both parents are fit . . . here it is."

"What?" Steve pleaded as Bennet took a moment to read on.

"Since the dissolution of the marriage, there has been a very substantial change in circumstances on a temporary basis, to wit the continued conflict of religions. The effect this conflict has on the child Bobby, the considerable alienation that has occurred from his mother, his identification with his father, all indicate there should be a temporary change from the present joint custody to temporary residential responsibility to be vested in the father with both parents retaining shared responsibility. This change is conditioned upon both parties and the child participating in family therapy. It's subject to review not earlier than December 15th of this year."

"What visitation does he recommend?" the father asked.

"Here it is," Bennet said. "During the period of family counseling the mother will have her weekly visitation at 5:00 p.m. every Friday to return the child to the father at 6:00 p.m. on Saturdays. The father should find some way for the child to eat non-kosher from Friday afternoon to Saturday evening or provide proper dietary food when Bobby is with his mother."

"She gets him for the Sabbath?! And what does he mean about finding some way for Bobby to eat non-kosher? Only God can change the dietary laws! Still, overall, it's a tremendous improvement over what I had," Steve said.

"Do you want me to file an exception about the Sabbath visitation?" the lawyer asked.

"I guess not. She has to get him sometime. If I give the boy to his mom on Sunday, she'll have him back in church. Royce wants to downplay religion on both sides but I can still take my son to the evening service at an Orthodox temple on Saturday. He gets to go to our Sunday school, and he'll be in the Hebrew class I teach on Thursday nights. We'll appear cooperative. Let Carmen's side file their exceptions. From here on, the burden has shifted to Schmidt's shoulders. Well done, Bennet. Just try to delete the phrase about eating non-kosher, and leave in the part about my providing proper dietary food for him while he's at his mom's home. How long do you think it will take for Judge Watts to sign the order, assuming he'll sign it at all?"

"About a week. Schmidt's ten days to file exceptions start from then, but don't be shocked if he files them earlier than that," Bennet warned.

"At this time," Steve said, "I don't think there's anything that can surprise me."

Bennet assumed that Steve knew enough about the law to understand what rules accompanied the filing of "exceptions." That turned out to be a poor assumption.

It took two and a half weeks for Watts to get around to signing the order. Robinson called the judge's secretary not less than five times, but the calls made Watts angry and only served to give him reason to put off the signing until he was "damn ready." At last, on a Friday afternoon, Bennet called his client to inform him that the deed was done and that he expected to have it in his office by the following Monday. It happened to be a normal visitation weekend for Steve so he drove over to pick up his son and give him the good news.

When Steve arrived at his ex-wife's home, she was gone and her husband was outside mowing the lawn. Robinson had never spoken with Ricardo before, and he didn't like to be put in the position of asking the fellow for the whereabouts of Bobby.

"His mama take him eshopping," the Latin said in broken English. "I no have no idea when they comma back."

That made Steve's blood boil. She knew full well that it was his weekend. Enraged, and worried that Carmen might abscond with the child, he drove off yelling that he'd be back soon enough with the cops.

The irate dad called his ex on Monday afternoon when he had the signed order in his hand. He wanted to know if Carmen would obey it. True to form, she told him that she wouldn't. At that point he took the order over to the Key Biscayne Police Department and requested their assistance in enforcing it. There was some confusion and reluctance on their part at first, but when he threatened a lawsuit if they refused to "do their duty and enforce the law," they decided that they'd do their best to get him his son.

The police prepositioned two unmarked cars near her home, in spots where they could quickly block off any escape. Then a sergeant called Mrs. Estavan and pleaded with her to obey the law. She hung up on him, grabbed her child and raced for the car. By the time she got the garage door open and had started to back out, the cops were all over the place and had blocked her attempt to pull back into the garage. They showed her the order, but she produced another one, that which had been signed years before to originally give her primary residency. "Yes," the sergeant said sympathetically, "but this one's newer and replaces that old thing. You'll have to turn the boy over." While all this was going on, Steve sat nearby in a patrol car as Bobby was jumping up and down for joy, sure that he was finally going to be living with his daddy. The two waved to each other, and Steve tried to reassure him by giving him the "thumbs up" sign. Finally, with the first true tears that Steve had ever seen her shed, Carmen agreed to release her son. Bobby ran to his father shouting "yippee." Though the taste of victory seemed sweet indeed, the father was able to empathize for the woman as he drove off. He remembered that a month after Carmen had pulled out in 1978, denying him visitation rights, he had forcibly taken his son from Theresa's house, only to wind up handing the child back to the police a few hours later.

In the car Bobby learned the details of the court order for the first time, as his mother had denied him access to his father from the day that it had been issued until then.

"It sounds pretty good, Dad. But I don't like the part about missing Friday nights. How am I gonna see Rachel?" he asked. Rachel was the rabbi's daughter, and though Bobby was just seven, and she was only six, the two had already "promised each other their hands in marriage."

"I wouldn't worry too much about that if I were you, son. Look, the order covers only a six-month period. I'm sure the visitation will eventually change. In the meantime, it's important for you to be nice to your mom. The order says that each parent must foster a loving attitude by you to the other parent."

"I don't want to see mom at all anymore," Bobby said.

"I don't believe that for a moment, Bobby, and even if it were true, you'd better know that an attitude like that might result in the court awarding final custody right back with her again."

"I hate her and she hates me," the boy said.

"That's not true. Your mother loves you."

"Then why'd she baptize me?"

"Any good mother would do whatever she thought necessary to try to hold on to her child," he answered.

Bobby said he understood and promised to be well-behaved when his mother had visitation. The two then went home to celebrate.

— 19 —
SETBACKS

Nothing worthwhile in life is ever easy. Steve's joy lasted all the way until the next morning when he received a call from his attorney. Bennet told him that Schmidt had called for an emergency hearing before Judge Watts to protest the heavy-handed way the father had removed his child from the mother's home. More, he was claiming that Steve had no right to take the boy before the exceptions were filed. In fact, Bennet pointed out, the order said (in small print) "subject to timely exceptions." The lawyer still hadn't explained the meaning of the phrase to Steve, and the police hadn't understood its significance either in aiding the father to take his son. By this time, Schmidt had indeed filed exceptions to the order, thirty-five in all. He had raised constitutional questions of the separation of Church and State, and it was now apparent that, short of Divine intervention, this case was headed for the Supreme Court.

All the key parties had to appear before the judge the next day. Steve was on summer active duty with the Coast Guard Reserves and was serving at the Federal Building across the street from the County Courthouse. He took

Bobby to work with him that morning and prayed that he wouldn't have to hand his son back after two short days of possession. Both father and son were highly distraught over the prospect of another forced separation. During the hearing, Robinson left his boy (dressed in a miniature Coast Guard uniform) with his boss, Rosa Lee Boatright, an understanding woman who had once herself been through the courts in a fight for custody of a child.

Outside the judge's chambers the opposing parties were confined to a small hallway. Steve felt like punching out everybody on the other side, especially Ricardo who was financing the drive to steal his son again. He couldn't understand why any man would want to fight so hard to get custody of a kid that hated his guts. Still, he knew that he had to keep his cool, and he did.

The parties were called in as Watts sneered, "What's this case about? Oh yea, I read about it in the paper. I think it's disgraceful the way the two of you've been acting."

"What's disgraceful, Your Honor," Schmidt replied, "is the religious war that Mr. Robinson has subjected my client to. Now that man has managed to humiliate Mrs. Estavan by bringing half the Key Biscayne Police Department down on her house as if she were some type of common criminal. They have illegally removed the minor child in question from her home. Your order, signed last Friday, states that it's subject to timely exceptions. As Your Honor is well aware, I had ten days to file exceptions, and I did so yesterday, well within the prescribed time limit. In fact, I filed 35 exceptions to the general master's report, which violates a number of times the concept of separation between Church and State."

"Let me assure you, Your Honor," Bennet interrupted, "that had I known of my client's intention, I would have warned him against it."

"Your Honor," Steve broke in, "may I make a statement?" The judge nodded yes, and Robinson continued, "That woman had, for the past several weeks, denied me of all visitation with my son. Not only that but . . ." He wanted to tell the judge about Carmen's previous contempt of court, of her pledge to disobey the judge's order, but he never got the chance.

"But nothing!" Watts bellowed. "Young man, you will hand over the boy to his mother *forthright*! And both of you will live in accordance with my original custody and visitation order dated January, 1981, until *all* appeals have been heard. When all is said and done, you may well gain primary residency, Mr. Robinson. But you must wait for the legal process to run its course!"

Steve asked his lawyer to do something about the visitation. General Master Royce had extended his rights to include a Monday return of the boy after weekend stays, and Watts' old order would cut it again to Sunday night.

"The judge is in no mood to listen to us. Grin and bear it, we'll get 'em on the appeals hearing," Bennet advised.

"How soon can you give Mr. Schmidt a hearing on his exceptions?" Bennet asked.

"In three weeks I have a number of openings. Here's one: August 9th. I'll give you an hour. In the interim I except both parties to live fully by my original order. I don't know how you got the police department to assist you in this insanity, but I warn you . . . don't try something like that again."

Schmidt tried to make an allegation about Steve's falling behind in child-support payments ever since the general master's report had been released, but Watts would listen to none of it during the five-minute hearing.

As they left the judge's chambers, Schmidt murmured to Bennet, "Christ, I wish they'd just put the kid on the stand already and let him say what he wants." Any lawyer who's put in the position of fighting for a cause he doesn't believe in must eventually have second thoughts about his job. Schmidt was aware of how Bobby felt from all he had heard, and he was smart enough to know the impact that the judge's new order would have on the lad, who was beginning to feel like a yo-yo. The remark caught Steve by surprise though, for he had viewed the attorney as a heartless neo-Nazi until that moment. "If the man thinks that way, then how could he morally justify covering up for his client's contempt of court?" he thought.

The next few moments were among the toughest of the father's life. He had to walk across the street and tell his son that he must go back to his mother and suffer reduced visitation until the ordeal was over. When Bobby heard about it, he broke down and started to cry. At that moment he had more hatred for his mother than he'd ever felt before. Steve tried to explain the reason for the quick return, but he couldn't. "Look, Bobby," he said, "I don't like it anymore than you do. But in this country, we live by laws and for today, not forever, the law says that you go back to your mother. Believe me, it doesn't end here. There's another hearing in just a few weeks. We'll know more then. The burden of proof will be on your mother to show that the general master was wrong."

Bobby stepped into his mother's car as it started to rain. He told her how he felt about her. All she could say in return was, "Some day you'll know how much I love you and you'll thank me for what I'm doing." At that moment a lightning bolt struck a tree next to their parked car. It was pouring by now and it seemed that even the heavens wept for the agony of "Moshe Ben Ithamar Halevi."

"I'll never thank you and I'll never love you," Bobby replied and added, "Look at the lightning. God is watching you and He knows you're wrong."

Wrong or not, she had him again that Wednesday. Steve's next visitation period started five hours later, but it was a much different reunion than it had been two days before.

Robinson spent the following days trying to raise more money to keep up with his escalating legal expenses. He had still been writing most of the pleadings himself, but was now paying three attorneys for advice which was getting expensive. To be sure, the Jewish attorneys didn't charge him for all the work they were doing. They all wanted to see their "little Moses" freed, and Busker in particular had done a lot of work at no cost in the early stages of the battle. But Robinson found it worthwhile to retain the man who quickly discovered a highly pertinent case to refute some of Schmidt's exceptions. In Vazquez vs. Vazquez, a 1983 Florida case, the two parents agreed to raise a child Catholic. They had him baptized into that faith, but when the mother moved out she started taking her son to a Baptist church. The father objected, saying that the kid was baptized Catholic in accordance with the original agreement. Although Mrs. Vazquez claimed that she had a right to expose him to her new faith, the judge said that the original agreement had priority over her recent interest, and ruled in favor of the father. If that original agreement was enforced by the Court, then the precedence had been set to honor the value of the Brith Milah agreement, too.

A week before the next court date, the H.R.S. social worker filed his report with the court. It wasn't the sort of news that Steve had been hoping for, for while its overall recommendations were ambiguous, its general tone was violently hostile towards Robinson. Still, as Schmidt had stipulated to a decision by the general master based solely upon testimony of psychologists Goldberg and Gray, there was hope that the affect of the new report could be overcome.

On August 9th, the parties filed back into the courtroom again so Schmidt could argue his 35 exceptions to the general master's report. As the court reporter set up, Watts looked out at Robinson and sarcastically said, "You again! I remember trying this case years ago. You're the fellow who ran off to Israel for a year and left his wife and child without any support! What are you shaking your head about?"

"Your Honor," Steve answered, "your memory is in error. I took a six-week vacation in Israel, not a year's leave, some five months after my ex left me, taking the child and essentially denying me almost all visitation."

"I knew it was something like that," Watts angrily replied. "I want everybody present to know that I have no intention of making any decision here based on religious matters. I didn't consider religion when I made my original ruling, and I don't care about it now. I think this whole thing is a disgrace, especially you, young man, putting a child Bobby's age up on the pulpit to preach. I want both sides to understand that I will *not* receive any new testimony today. We are here to discuss law, and I want all sides to focus on that alone. Now, Mr. Schmidt, I believe that these exceptions are yours. You may begin."

"I've cited a number of important cases in my brief, Your Honor," Schmidt began, "and as you have undoubtedly read by now, there are a number of cases to show that the wishes of a child Bobby's age do not have to be considered when awarding custody. The boy is barely beyond what is normally termed tender years, and he's certainly not close to being twelve, the age when a child has the right, within reason, to specify to a court where he wishes to reside. More, the findings of the general master are a clear violation of the separation of Church and State. This order is insane! How would Your Honor like someone to come into your house and demand that you keep a kosher home? This order will produce the further alienation of the boy from his mom by demanding that he eat food which is different from what she would eat! On top of all this, when you originally awarded primary residency to the mother, you gave the father liberal visitation; but with this order, the mother goes from having primary residency down to having the child with her only 25 hours per week. Why should the mother be so restricted now? What's more, there's no provision here for holidays or summer visitation beyond one day per week. What you are doing with this order is to reward the father for alienating the boy from his mother. If the father has been so successful in turning the child against his mother with his current visitation, imagine how much more he will destroy the mother-son relationship when her time with the boy is reduced to one day per week! Then there's the issue of what religion the boy should be. The attempt to admit testimony from the mohel in the form of a deposition was denied by General Master Royce. There's not one shred of evidence in admission with this Court to show that the mother ever promised to raise this boy in the Jewish faith. In fact, in Jewish law it's the mother who determines the religion of the child, not the father. Indeed, that's what Mr. Robinson told my client when they met.

"Your Honor, we've just received the report of the H.R.S. social worker on this case, and it fully reveals what type of man Mr. Robinson is. I quote: 'This reporter has spent some 25 years interviewing children for the Dade County courts. In all that time, I cannot ever remember meeting a child so brainwashed as this one. The father must spend every waking moment with the child indoctrinating him as to his ideas about religion, women and marriage. The father has stated to this writer that this child is the only child there at the synagogue and consequently he is thrown in with adults. The child uses the Torah for his own benefit. He says Torah tells him that he cannot eat bacon and ham, but when asked by me if Torah says anything about honoring thy mother and thy father, the conversation was instantly changed to another subject. The sadness in this case is that the child's viewpoint has been so distorted about what is right and what is wrong, what is a child's responsibility and what is an adult's responsibility, that if he does not get some therapy as quickly as possible there may be some long-range damage done to him. At this point whatever the father does is perfectly all right with Bobby, but anything the mother does is going to be wrong."

"These, Your Honor, are my strongest exceptions to the Order and Report of the General Master. The others are listed in my brief along with numerous relevant cases to show the error of the report from a legal viewpoint." Schmidt then rested.

"Mr. Cohen, how say you?" the judge asked.

"Well, as you have seen, Your Honor, we've found our own relevant cases, especially Vazquez vs. Vazquez, a 1983 Florida case that bears a great deal of similarity to this one, where the court found that the original agreement between parents which could be documented could not be overturned with the conversion of one of the parents to a new faith. Bobby Robinson was circumcised with a brith milah, and the court file from 1981 includes a copy of the circumcision certificate."

"I don't see what's the big deal about the boy being circumcised. Lots of people are circumcised and it doesn't prove anything," the judge asserted.

"You don't understand, Your Honor," Bennet replied. "It's true that many Christian baby boys are now circumcised, but a brith milah is a religious ceremony, not a mere medical procedure. Bobby was circumcised by a member of the Jewish clergy, not by a doctor.

"And as for the social worker's report, the bottom line states: The recommendation of the psychologist should be heeded! Well, the court-appointed psychologist plainly recommended that primary residency should be, on a trial basis, vested with the father!"

"I have your briefs, and I don't think I need to hear anymore today. Mr. Schmidt, have you brought a transcript of the hearing before General Master Royce for me to review?" Watts asked.

"I have, Your Honor. Here it is."

"I'm going on vacation tomorrow so I won't get to this for some time. Mr. Robinson, I don't want you calling my secretary and pestering her about my decision as you have in the past. I'll give you my answer sometime in the future. Good day."

At that, the hearing broke up and Steve just sat there with a very empty feeling. So much of what he had heard seemed so unfair, downright bigoted in fact. Bennet saw it the same way, especially the judge's opening remarks. Still, the attorney was optimistic that Schmidt wouldn't be able to show "clearly erroneous" which was necessary to overturn Royce's recommendations.

The conversation shifted to the Archdiocese of Miami. Steve wanted to know if his attorney had heard anything from the Church. He hadn't, so Robinson asked him to prepare the suit against them. "Are you crazy?" Bennet asked, "You can't beat the Vatican! Besides, Watts is still on the case!"

"I told you before . . . there's more to this case than Bobby alone. Rome has defecated on me, my family and my people, and now they probably think they've gotten away with it because they haven't heard from us in weeks. I want my pound of flesh," Steve said.

"You want to sue the Church," Bennet said, "sue them. You know how to write pleadings and lawsuits by now. If I file the thing, I'll lose all my Catholic clients."

"When I hired you, I told you that I wanted you to handle both the custody issue and the Church problem," Robinson argued.

"I'm sorry. I can't recommend that you sue the Church at this time, and I don't care about any contingency fee that may or may not be ten years off by the time this thing hits the Supreme Court."

"All right," Steve said, "I'll wait a few more weeks. But come September if I don't get any satisfaction, I'm gonna file. It'll take me a few weeks to put the suit together anyway. Can I count on you to at least answer my questions while I write the thing?"

Bennet told him that he could, within limits. "Are you gonna use that Holocaust stuff?" the attorney wanted to know. The answer, of course, was "yes."

"Don't you realize," Bennet then asked, "that the majority of any jury is likely to be Christian?"

Steve knew that, but figured that "Christian" didn't necessarily mean "Catholic." There were many Protestants who were just as opposed to the Vatican as he was. With a little luck and creative jury selection, he hoped to land that type Christian along with a few Jews on the jury. His attack would be against the papacy, not Catholics or Christianity itself.

"But why include the Nazi connection?" Bennet asked.

"To win the way I want to win I have to go for punitive damages. One priest throwing water on a kid's head is, by itself, not worth much, let alone six million dollars. To go for a symbolic figure like that I've got to demonstrate that what was done was part of a continuing war that the Vatican has conducted against the Jews. From the First Crusade in 1096 through Torquemada's Spanish Inquisition of 1492 to the 1569 order to expel Jews from Papal States to the Papal Concordat with Hitler, Jewish persecution has been a favorite Papal pastime. This pope even invited Arafat, arch enemy of the Jews, to Rome. He won't recognize Israel as a sovereign nation, but the P.L.O., who's charter calls for the destruction of Israel . . . the P.L.O., supreme terrorist organization of the world, he will! Vatican persecution of the Jews is not ancient history. It is, on the part of Rome, an ongoing process, and it is for this reason that I think the courts will be open to giving Rome a symbolic kick in the gluteus maximus. By the way, speaking of a kick in the posterior, in the 1800's that's what the pope did to the chief rabbi of Rome in public every Easter because we haven't accepted Christ."

Bennet remained unconvinced, but Steve Busker was not. He wanted to help, but advised his client to get an expert in Constitutional law to give him a hand. Both attorneys warned him again not to do anything rash.

A few weeks passed. Robinson continued to boil over the remarks that Watts had made. He called the B'nai Brith Antidefamation League and the A.C.L.U. about the comments to find out if there wasn't some way to get the judge off the bench. B'nai Brith was no help at all, but the A.C.L.U. promised to take the case if the judge ruled against him, for they too saw the remarks as bigoted. Still, Steve wasn't content to just sit and wait.

Bob Finnerty, Robinson's old friend who was an expert in his own right when it came to filing legal pleadings, flew into town on the way to a gambling paraphernalia convention at the Breakers Hotel in Palm Beach. He listened to Steve's story and suggested that his friend file an "Affidavit of Prejudice" with the Court.

"Your lawyer won't tell you this," Bob said, "because

the Motion to Disqualify Trial Judge is an insult to any judge and attorneys don't like to tick off men they must plead cases before over and over again, but most judges will honor the Motion and get off the case right away. Do it. Watts'll fold. I can almost guarantee it."

Steve took the idea to his attorneys. They thought it made good sense, but as Finnerty had suggested, they wanted no part in the Motion themselves. It would have to be drawn up by Robinson, though Bennet promised to accompany him to court to deliver it.

There was a problem about witnesses to the remarks which had to be overcome before the thing might fly. Still, Bennet promised to do his best to get the judge to accept the Motion based on "the equities of the situation." He felt that Watts would probably go along with it because, as a politician, he was uncomfortable with a case this controversial.

— 20 —
THE FINAL ROUND

A hearing on the Motion to Disqualify Trial Judge was set for September 18th. Robinson hadn't been idle as that date approached. He had not only prepared the Motion, but a hundred-page lawsuit to be filed against the Church, naming everyone from the priest who had carried out the baptism right up to the Pope himself. The suit was ready by September 14th. The angry dad wasted no time in phoning the *Herald* and the attorneys for the Archdiocese to tell them that it was going to be filed on September 24th unless the baptism was annulled by that day at 9:00 a.m. He made certain that Fitzpatrick understood the thrust of his attack would be to link the Vatican to the Holocaust and promised to rip the Church wide open with "new evidence." In reality, all he had was what had already been filed in his custody proceedings, but he thought that was more than enough to do the job, and he knew it was best to keep his opponent off guard. Anyway, if a cursory search of the 1933 *New York Times* microfilm copies could reveal so much, it was almost certain that the Church itself was sitting on far more incriminating evidence that it had to fear might leak out one day.

On Monday, September 17th, Steve called Fitzpatrick back to remind him that his Church had seven days to comply. On Tuesday, the 18th, he called again to tell him it was now down to six days.

Tuesday was also "D Day" (or Dump Watts Day) for Robinson. Only four people showed up to see the judge: Steve, Bennet Cohen, Karl Schmidt and Carmen.

Bennet was first to speak after the preliminaries.

"Your Honor," he began, "my client's here today with an Affidavit in Support of his Motion to Disqualify Trial Judge. Before he speaks, and I want to make clear that this is *his* doing, I would like to address some problems that I'm sure Mr. Schmidt will bring up. As Your Honor is aware, in Florida Civil law there are two witnesses required to support accusations of prejudicial remarks made by a judge if the strict letter of the law is to be followed. The equity of the situation, however, demands that civil procedure be set aside. On the day that the alleged remarks were made by you, there were no witnesses save myself, my associates, and Mr. Schmidt, all attorneys, prohibited by the statute from serving as witnesses. Mrs. Estavan was present, but she can hardly be called as a witness by our side. There was a court reporter, but we ask you to spare Mr. Robinson the expense of requiring a transcript. Instead, we ask that you do justice to the Motion by searching your own memory as to what transpired that day. Mr. Robinson, tell the judge why you want to disqualify him."

Steve took a deep breath as if to get up the courage and then began. "Your Honor, as I stated in my Affidavit, I fear that I may not receive a fair decision in this proceeding due to apparent prejudice or bias on your part."

"How so?" the judge asked.

"There are six points I would like to address."

"Proceed," Watts said.

"You stated at the onset of the last hearing that you remembered trying the case originally. You then falsely accused me of abandoning my wife and child to run off to Israel for a year. When I corrected you and told you that some five months after my wife left me, I took a six-week vacation in Israel to calm my nerves, you said, 'Oh well, I knew it was something like that.' Needless to say, there is a vast difference between a man abandoning his family for a year, and a man taking a six-week vacation five months after his wife has left him. I would add that I sent child support payments for my boy while I was in Israel. You acted like there were no differences between the two situations and you unfairly implied that I was negligent in my family responsibilities. That was my first concern. Second, you said at the onset of the hearing that you wouldn't consider religion in this case. Yet, as the press and the court-appointed psychologist have pointed out, religion is at the very core of this case. Dr. Goldberg has testified that the child in question has been beaten and deprived of food by his mother. The boy wishes to practice the religion that his mother swore before God Almighty to raise him in at his ritual circumcision or brith milah. His mother and step-father have conducted nothing short of a religious war against him. You can no more overlook religion in this case than you can in any other religious war. It is the sole problem that brought us here. Third, you stated in reference to ritual circumcision that, 'lots of people are circumcised.'"

"Well, they are," Watts retorted.

"That's true, but not by a member of the Jewish clergy for religious reasons. Circumcision is one of the cardinal precepts of the Jewish faith. It's been central to our religion ever since God instructed our forefather Abraham to make it a sign of the covenant between Him, God that is, and the Jewish people. You seemed to downgrade the entire practice to a simple medical procedure. We don't circumcise for medical reasons in Judaism. We do it as an act of our faith and love for God. If a Jew has the sign of God inscribed there, and understands what it means, he is reminded of God before he uses it to draw a soul into the world. This makes him less likely to commit an act of adultery, homosexuality, or incest. It tells him the purpose for all sexual pleasure. Fourth, you stated that you thought it was a disgrace that I would have Bobby 'preach from the pulpit.' You thus implied that my son has no right to freedom of religion or freedom of speech."

"That's your interpretation," Watts complained.

"Yes, it is," Steve said, "and it's my son's interpretation, too. Anyway, he doesn't preach. He sings Hebrew prayers to our God, and I believe that the Constitution guarantees him that right. Fifth, you said at the onset of the last hearing that you wouldn't receive testimony. That wasn't only fair. It was mandated by the agreement reached between all parties before General Master Royce when both sides stipulated to a decision based solely on the testimony of psychologists Goldberg and Gray. I waived a very large list of witnesses in agreeing to that. Mr. Schmidt knew full well what he was doing, too, and so did Mrs. Estavan. But you violated both your own instructions and our stipulation agreement by allowing Mr. Schmidt to read to the Court from the social worker's report. That report was never admitted as evidence, nor did we get the chance to cross-examine the man who wrote it. I'd like you to know that the writer of the report had told me that he had seen my indictment of the Vatican before he came to my house on the day he interviewed my family, that he told me he was Catholic, that he implied he was upset that I would link the Vatican with the Holocaust, and that he then proceeded to argue theology with my seven-year-old son as is evident by the Torah remarks that are included in his report. Finally, Your Honor, you said at the conclusion of the August 9th hearing that you'd give us your answer 'sometime in the future.' From the tone of your voice, you seemed to suggest that you might table the decision for a long, long time."

"Don't you think I'm entitled to a vacation?" Watts asked sarcastically.

"Yes, you're entitled. But it's now been forty days since the hearing and, unfortunately, my son can't take a vacation from the persecution he's suffering in his mother's home. You've had almost seven weeks to review the transcripts. Have you done so?"

"No," the judge admitted, "I seem to have lost them right after the hearing. I asked my secretary to look for them, but she hasn't come up with them yet. Mr. Schmidt, can you get me another copy?"

"Certainly, Your Honor," the attorney answered.

"The general master," Steve said, "after having heard the facts, ruled that it was neither desirable nor safe to leave Bobby in the care of his mother for more than one day per week. He reached that decision on June 29th, some twelve weeks ago, and yet this matter drags on and on and you don't know where you've placed the transcripts seven weeks ago. My kid's going nuts while this Court drags its feet. For all these reasons, I respectfully request that you step down from the case and let the chief judge assign it to another judge. Thank you for hearing me out."

"Mr. Schmidt, have you got something to say about this matter?" the judge asked.

"I think it's absolutely outrageous that *THAT* man can come in here and make such obscene accusations against a man who is as respected on the bench as Your Honor is. I sat here on that day and I remember nothing of what he says. I think he must have a very active imagination and persecution complex, both of which are indicative of why he shouldn't have custody of the child in question. And as for his having the right to come in here in the first place, as Mr. Cohen has pointed out, two witnesses are required. Where are they? Mr. Robinson hasn't even supplied the transcripts from the hearing in question. Why hasn't he supplied them? Because he knows damn well that they'll show *NOTHING* of what's been alleged here today. And then there's the issue of my client's interests. My fee is $150 per hour. Who's going to pay my client's added expense to go all through a repeat of the last hearing with another judge? Mr. Robinson? I doubt it! It's unfair to ask my client to pay for another hearing. I would add, that after having read Mr. Robinson's Affidavit, that it doesn't comply with the Florida Statutes which state that the petitioner must state that, and I quote, 'the filer fears that he *WILL* not receive a fair decision.' Mr. Robinson states only that he fears he *MAY* not receive a proper decision. '*MAY*' is not the same as '*WILL*.' Thus the affidavit is no good."

The judge took off his glasses and gave Steve a hard look. "Mr. Robinson," he said, "although I'm not prejudiced against your case or your religion, I'm going to grant your Motion." With these words Steve felt a surge of relief rush through his whole body. The judge continued: "Both of you are fighting for your child, and whoever loses will probably think I was wrong, but if you already think so, then I'll step down so you'll believe that you can get a fair decision. I'll have you know that my daughter is married to a Jewish attorney. I have nothing against Jews. For all you or I know, I might've well ruled in your favor. Mr. Cohen, draw up the necessary papers, and I'll see to it that the case is reassigned."

With tears of joy in his eyes, Steve said, "Thank you, Your Honor," and the hearing was over.

Schmidt was furious as they left the room. "Put a muzzle on your client," he urged Bennet.

"He's listed as a co-counselor, and he's a damn good one at that," Bennet beamed.

"I never know who I'm fighting with in this case!" Schmidt barked.

"You're fighting with us both. We're a team," Bennet said. With that they parted while Schmidt continued to mumble to himself. After almost five long years, Robinson was free of Watts and the case was reassigned to Judge Gerstein.

Luck, after years behind a cloud, had finally emerged to shine on Steve with a warm and loving smile. For at the very moment that Robinson was being freed from the bondage of Watt's decrees, John Fitzpatrick was meeting with Archbishop McCarthy to warn him of the upcoming Robinson suit.

— 21 —
JUSTICE FROM ROME

The call from the Archdiocese attorney was waiting for Steve when he finished teaching his last class before lunch on September 19, 1984.

"Well, do we Tango and make a little nasty history in the courts, or do I get my letter?" Robinson asked.

"I'd love to take your deposition . . . but I'm afraid I'll never get the chance. You can have the letter this afternoon. Be at my office any time after 3:00 P.M."

Wednesday was still visitation for Steve, so he drove out to Carmen's place to pick up his son before heading over to claim his prize.

"What's new?" Bobby asked as he jumped into his father's car and threw a big hug around his dad.

"The question's not what's new, but what's *NEWS* and the answer, young man, is about to be *YOU*. The Church has agreed to annul your baptism, a first in almost two thousand years!"

"You mean they're gonna let me be a Jew?" Bobby asked with obvious joy.

"That's right!"

"And there's nothing Mom can do about it?"

"Not a thing in the world once we get that letter in our hands. We're goin' over to get it right now. That's not all, son. Judge Watts is off the case!"

Bobby was so happy that tears began to flow down his handsome face. At last the end was in sight.

The exchange of Release from Liability for the letter went without a hitch at the attorney's office. The Archbishop's letter was incredible. It supplied Robinson with all he wanted and a thousand times more. He read it once, twice, a dozen times again. God, he thought, what must have transpired in McCarthy's office to have him come down so strongly on my side? He closed his eyes and tried to imagine the scene.

"Good morning, John. What's this about Robinson bringing suit before the press?" McCarthy might have stated.

"My secretary got the message on Friday, and he's called a number of times since then to tell us that we have until the 24th to get the letter of annulment to him. I've brought copies of everything he's filed concerning us on his custody case. It's my opinion that he's a genuine threat to the Church interests everywhere. I think we should grant the devil his due before the Holocaust stuff hits the press," the attorney probably said.

"Monsignor, you met with the Pope briefly on this matter. What was his advice?" the imagined Archbishop asked.

"The Holy Father isn't anxious to annul any baptism, being afraid that we might be opening a Pandora's box. On the other hand, while he isn't thrilled about giving Mr. Robinson what he wants, he's even less enthusiastic about confronting the Jews in an American court on the issue of Vatican ties to the Third Reich. The material brought by Mr. Fitzpatrick today won't look good if bathed in the light of the modern press. I recommend annulment of the baptism for three reasons. First, the mother wasn't a practicing Catholic until the past few months. We need to send a message to our flock that baptism is a sacred act, not one designed to be used as a tool of revenge when a marriage ends up on the rocks as interfaith marriages generally do. I'm convinced that Mrs. Estavan baptized the child in question solely as an act of punishment for her ex-husband. Second, reports from the boy's catechism class indicate that Bobby was and is militantly Jewish, both before and after the baptism occurred. He has quoted the Scriptures in class in an effort to prove that our Lord was a false prophet. The boy's father is a religious author. It's obvious that he has imparted to the boy a good deal of his opposition to our Lord and our Church. I would recommend that we emphasize the child's psychological well-being when we explain our decision to the press. Third, from what I've read of Mr. Robinson's work, and from what I've observed of the man himself when we met last March, he's a fiery man in search of a way to break our Church. If we placate him, we may defuse him; but if we fight him in the courts, we may lose even if we win. The trial could take years and would draw out all our dirty laundry with respect to the Holocaust."

Yes, Steve thought, it probably went something like that (a television interview with Monsignor Walsh later that week seemed to confirm the hypothesis about McCarthy using Bobby's psychological well-being as an excuse to give him what he wanted).

The date on the letter, September 13th, was troubling. The Church had called him about the letter on September 19th. Steve's final ultimatum (coupled with a threat to reveal the Holocaust evidence) was delivered on September 14th. Was McCarthy trying to make it look like the decision was made *before* the threat was delivered? Who cared! He read the letter again:

"Dear Mr. Robinson:

It has been brought to my attention that Robert Altair Robinson was baptized at The Church of the Holy Ascension on March 4, 1984, at the request of his mother, Carmen Estavan. The father, Steven Lloyd Robinson, was not consulted prior to the fact and is now objecting. Our investigation reveals that the parents were divorced on September 26, 1980, and joint custody was awarded. Prior to and during the marriage, the mother had been a non-practicing Catholic and the father was Jewish. The child was circumcised in accordance with Jewish ritual and the mother agreed that he would be raised Jewish. After the divorce, the father began taking the child regularly to synagogue and Hebrew school. When the mother presented the child for Baptism, he was seven years of age. The priest was not aware that the mother had told the child that the Baptism would place a shield over him so that he would not go to hell. Nor was he aware that the child had not been advised that Baptism was a sacrament of initiation into the Catholic Church, that he had not been instructed in the truths of the faith, and that prior to the baptism and to this day, the child considers himself to be Jewish.

Had Father Murray been aware of the facts, the Baptism would not have been conducted. Indeed, being aware of the facts and having consulted with experts in Theology and Canon Law, it is my judgment that Robert Altair Robinson is not a member of the Roman Catholic Church. The Baptism was not valid and the records of the Church should be corrected to reflect that.

Very truly yours,
Edward A. McCarthy,
Archbishop of Miami"

There must have been some concern about the effect the letter would have on Carmen's chances to appeal General Master Royce's findings. But if there was, it wasn't apparent from anything that the Archbishop had written. Perhaps McCarthy was angered by a perception that Carmen had been careless and flippant in her use of the Holy Sacraments. Maybe he hoped that Steve would be less likely to continue his war against the Vatican if he handed Bobby over on a silver platter.

Robinson made two more stops before heading home that day to share his joyous news with Ruth; Bennet's office and Schmidt's. Bennet wasn't in just then, but Steve Busker was. Busker almost did cartwheels when he read it. "Unbelievable," he said, "you just broke the back of the biggest church in the world!"

"Not quite," the father said, "they're still worshipping a man, but I have at last gotten some justice from Rome. Now I'm going to find out if I can get some from Schmidt and his client, too."

Carmen's attorney refused to come out to greet the victor when Steve arrived, but he could hear the father boast out in the reception area. "Tell Mr. Schmidt," Robinson advised the secretary, "that it's futile for him to fight me anymore. I'll give Carmen good visitation *if* she ends her resistance now and hands Bobby over to me. If this isn't done *forthright*, there's a lot more in store for that dear lady."

As Steve drove away with his son, he was surprised to learn that the boy had never been to his mother's attorney's office before. Schmidt had fought for nine months to keep Bobby away from his father, but he'd never actually met the boy himself! Perhaps, Steve thought, it was because Carmen had told him from the beginning about Bobby's sentiment and the lawyer didn't have the stomach to face him.

As soon as the Robinsons were gone, Schmidt came out of hiding and read the letter. He then picked up the phone and called Carmen to give her the news, along with his decision to withdraw from the case, though he did offer to have his associate negotiate terms for an out-of-court settlement.

According to Bobby, his mother reacted to the Archbishop's letter by removing the crucifix from the wall in her bedroom, then throwing it into a bathroom in her garage (where it stayed for a year before being put up again).

There was a celebration at the Homestead Jewish Center

that night as word of their school director's success quickly spread throughout the congregation. Not having heard from Carmen by the following afternoon, Robinson set out to go for the "kill" by calling Arnold Markowitz of the *Miami Herald*, the new reporter assigned to the story. After hearing the letter read over the phone, Markowitz made him swear that he wouldn't give the story to anyone else before he could get it into the paper.

"Do you want me to print the threats to expose the Holocaust material?" the reporter asked.

"No. Make me come across as being grateful to the Church for honoring my son's right to religious freedom, and my rights as a parent with joint custody. I hope this decision marks a turning point in the relationship between Jews and the Catholic Church. Emphasize the positive."

"It's easy to be gracious when you're a winner," the reporter remarked.

"I'm not finished with Rome yet, but this isn't the time for sour grapes. In due time the full story will be told. A newspaper article, however, can never do it justice. I'll write a book about it, perhaps using the first person, perhaps using the third, or feed the story to some other author."

"Why do you think it's necessary to do that?" Markowitz asked.

"While I appreciate what the Church has done, I believe they did it only because they feared the adverse publicity about the Holocaust, not because they were truly concerned about Bobby's well-being. Besides, I don't have the right to sit on the evidence I've uncovered any more than I would have the right to remain silent if I witnessed any other murder. A heinous crime has been committed and there's blood on Rome's hands. The truth must come out."

"Do you think the boy's mother will talk to me?" Markowitz asked.

"Would you if you were in her place?" Steve responded.

Markowitz promised to do his best to get the story into the *Herald* on the following day, Friday, September 21st. He did . . . on page one. The story, entitled CATHOLICS ANNUL BAPTISM OF UNINFORMED JEWISH BOY, was two pages long. There was a big picture of his son on the first page with a caption under it reading, "Robert Robinson considers himself a Jew." In the article Monsignor Walsh was quoted as saying, "For the mother to promote the sacrament as a protective shield against hell was doctrinally wrong, an idea he had not heard before, possibly as a reassuring but badly oversimplified description of baptism's salvation aspects."

Walsh also said, "The rules include making sure a child who has reached the age of reason knows what he is doing, does it freely, and has an understanding of the Catholic faith adequate for his age." As for the age of reason, he did not mention that Bobby was still six weeks short of his seventh birthday when the baptism occurred. Seven was the age of reason as defined by the Church.

As for Father Murray, the Archdiocese chose to reprimand him before the world. Monsignor Walsh blamed the priest's lack of experience for his failure to learn Robert's background and to make sure he understood the meaning of baptism. It seemed that McCarthy wanted to insure that his priests would learn from his example. Priests would now have to be more careful before baptizing the children of interfaith marriages and divorces. Father Murray was transferred away from his beloved church.

Rabbi Goldin was also quoted in the *Herald*. He said, "Judaism holds a deep institutional concern about dishonest baptisms. We have a sad history over the years where Jewish children were baptized by those of Christian faiths because they wanted to save the Jewish soul. We don't hear about it today, but the history is fresh enough in our collective conscience to make us extremely sensitive."

Steve first learned that the news had been published so fast when his fellow teachers began to congratulate him at work. Carmen got the word when she saw her son's face staring back at her from the paper on her doorstep that morning. She nearly passed out. It's one thing to lose a custody battle, but quite another to have the loss broadcast to the world.

By the end of the day Steve, his wife and his son had appeared on CNN and numerous local news programs. One broadcast showed Bobby singing the *Kiddush* prayer in Hebrew. The young man didn't neglect to take the on-camera opportunity to thank the Archbishop for "letting me be a Jew and making the Baptism as though it were nothing at all."

By Saturday, September 22, the story had shown up in the *New York Times*, the *New York Daily News*, and in Philadelphia, Houston, Los Angeles, and San Francisco newspapers. It even appeared in the *Weekly World News*, a tabloid that was generally occupied with tales of Big Foot or U.F.O. invasions.

On the following Monday morning, Bennet received a call from Karl Schmidt. Bennet didn't know what to expect at first. He worried about a new suit based on all the publicity. Schmidt's message, however, was short. "Please tell Mr. Robinson that he has my personal respect. You may also tell him that my client is now ready to come to terms."

EPILOGUE

As the years rolled by, Bobby (with his mother's consent) and Ruth, studying under the direction of Rabbi Ralph Glixman, both earned Orthodox conversions.

Archbishop McCarthy and the Archdiocese of Miami stepped up efforts to improve Catholic-Jewish relations. Steve found himself hoping the Archbishop of Miami would one day become the Bishop of Rome.

Robinson persisted in his efforts to try to reach out to Arab organizations like the P.L.O. in an attempt to fulfill his messianic vision of a Temple for Israel and a nation for the Palestinians. However, with time and a string of unanswered letters, he began to feel that (despite the P.L.O.'s endorsement of U.N. 242) the "Arafats" of this world are interested only in creating problems, not in finding solutions.

Over the next four years there were a series of meetings between Steve and Rabbi Shoulson.

"Am I the gilgol of Sabbatai Sevi?" the rabbi was asked.

"I can't say that you are, and I can't say that you're not," the rabbi said. "However, I can say that the importance of this life is always to be emphasized over any possible past life. What are your plans?"

"I don't know if I'm really the reincarnation of Sevi either, but the similarities are striking and God has allowed me to alter the doctrine of Christianity's prime Church at least once. If I am Sabbatai Sevi, God will make His will known to me.

"I must ensure that the story is told and preach the Temple-trade idea. If the rabbis of the world find merit in a reborn, repentant Sabbatai Sevi and if they're willing to discuss my concept of a peace settlement, God will see that they find me. He'll give me the strength needed to break through the Qelippoth (evil shells) that surround my soul. That could enable me to aid in establishing God's Kingdom on earth. If not, well, I'll live out the rest of my life content with the knowledge of what's been done for me. Who knows," he said with a laugh, "perhaps I'll achieve His purpose in some future incarnation."

"The land of Israel is God's gift to our people. How can we ever give even a part of it up?" Shoulson asked.

"God gave us food, and laws to offer some of it back through sacrifice. God gave us Israel. If we really want peace, then we've got to offer some of it back, too. The time has come for us to choose. Either we live like other nations and put our love for land and power first, or earn our Chosen status by showing the world that our Temple and our desire to fulfill God's laws are paramount."

"The Torah gives *all* of Israel to our people," Shoulson argued.

"The Israel that exists today is but a shadow of the Israel of Messianic times. There are some Orthodox here and in

Israel who don't even recognize the State of Israel because the Messiah has yet to come, something that for ages has been seen by our people as a pre-condition for Israel's full restoration. As for the Torah, the Israel it describes is far greater than the Israel of today. Its borders extend from Lebanon to the Euphrates River in Iraq. (Deuteronomy 11:24.)

"The true Israel will begin to come into being only with the re-establishment of the Temple, which will act as a focal point for God's power. Israel's borders will be set not by man, but by God at that time."

"What evidence do you cite for that?" the rabbi asked.

"In Exodus 34:24 God told us that he would cast out the nations before us, and enlarge our territory. He further said that no one will covet our land. But *when* will this happen? The verse says that it will happen when we 'go up to appear before the Lord our God three times a year,' the three times that we offer sacrifice in the Temple. That means we must *first* rebuild the Temple and reinstate the practice of Torah-ordained sacrifice, then worry about Israel's borders. Israel has nuclear weapons, including the neutron bomb. It can, even with smaller borders, provide for its own security until the time that God Himself seeks to intervene. I don't say give up every square inch of conquered West Bank territory. Keep what is needed for security. But give up what is needed to get the Temple back and to establish peace.

"One thing is for sure, the verse describes a time when Gentiles will not 'covet' the land. Such a change in attitude implies a new order. It may involve massive conversions to Judaism, or it may involve inspiring our Muslim cousins to live in accordance with the loving aspects of Mohammed's revelation. Islam has not yet safeguarded Beirut, or kept Iranians and Iraqis from firing missiles into each other's cities, or from using gas warfare to wipe out thousands. We must use a rebuilt Temple to help restore them as equals in the family of Abraham. An Israel, complete with Temple and dedicated to peace for all mankind, may well inspire the change in human nature described by the Torah. We *must* work to establish such an Israel.

"Negotiations between Shamir and Arafat can't accomplish the kind of change required to achieve a meaningful peace. The problem at hand is more religious than political, and as such, what's necessary is a leader who can bring the top rabbis and Moslem leaders of the world together into the kind of dialogue needed to end the coveting of the land spoken of by the Torah."

There was discussion of a joint venture to produce a movie about the custody battle (for Shoulson was already, by chance, involved in making films); but, after several meetings had taken place, it became apparent that the rabbi's health was not up to serious pursuit of such a project. The rabbi did, however, make an effort to find an editor for Steve's manuscript, though an unsuccessful one. There was fear that a book revealing the truth of the custody battle would cause an increase of anti-Semitism.

"I would hope," Steve said, "that America is a better nation than what you fear, but I must point out that, should our people be driven out of this land, we have long known that one of the signs of the Messianic Age is the *full* return of our people to Israel. At any rate, God did not split the Red Sea to lead us unto New York or Miami Beach. And as for the Christians, I have heard fundamentalists like Jerry Falwell often preach on television that Jesus cannot return until we Jews rebuild our Temple. Such Christians will support my proposal for a peace settlement. We can challenge them to see who's right about the identity of the Messiah. If they're right, they'll get their Jesus, and if we're right, we'll have our hopes fulfilled. Both faiths want A Messish, whoever he is. Let's set the stage and let God answer the age-old question once and for all."

In 1987 Steve took his wife and son to Israel. If he was still skeptical about the transmigration of souls before the trip, once again it was Ruth who managed to sway him. While visiting Yad Vashem, Israel's Holocaust Memorial Museum, the Korean convert reacted with such intense hysteria to a room full of children's shoes . . . shoes from the children of the gas chambers and the ovens, that she left no question in his mind that she had been one of those children.

"I don't want to see those shoes!" she screamed with horror as she ran from the building. It was then that he remembered his own feeling of panic at the train station in Hamburg in 1979. It was then that he understood . . . You can kill the body of a Jew . . . but you can never kill the soul of a Jew. God had sacrificed Jewish flesh to regain his beloved Israel, but he had restored the souls to new bodies, bodies whose brains had somehow managed to keep the horrid memories simmering just below the level of outright conscious thought. The souls that were there at Sinai, were there again at Auschwitz . . . and the souls that were there at Auschwitz, are here again today, an everlasting reminder to the world of its sin.

Convinced that he could not have won custody the way he had unless his prayer at Sinai had been heard, Steve also returned to the holy mountain with Ruth and Bobby. There, on sacred ground, Robinson gave thanks and again asked the Lord to let him know His will. Only time will show the results of that prayer.

Author Barry Steven Roffman

ABOUT THE AUTHOR

Born in Philadelphia, Pennsylvania, in 1947, Mr. Roffman is a 1969 graduate of Temple University. He was (for ten years) an officer in the Naval Reserve, having served on aircraft carriers, destroyers, a mine sweeper and an amphibious communications command ship.

In 1983 Mr. Roffman switched to the Coast Guard where he has since served in Alameda, California; Adak, Alaska; and Miami, Florida, as a Defense Readiness Planner. His current duties include the writing of defense (war) plans and frequent participation in war games on both Atlantic and Pacific Coasts. As such, he sometimes finds himself back at sea on Navy ships, working as an exercise controller or evaluator.

While in Miami, the author became an Orthodox Jew. He has recently assumed a position as acting director of B'Nai Israel, a synagogue in South Dade. When not writing war plans or helping out with his synagogue, Mr. Roffman enjoys traveling and flying as a private pilot.

For additional copies of *A Matter Of Spiritual Custody* by Barry Steven Roffman send $17.50 (postpaid) to:

Rainbow Books,
P.O. Box 1069,
Moore Haven, FL 33471
or telephone (813) 946-0293.
(Mastercard and Visa accepted.)